Behind the Wall

Behind the Wall

My brother, my family and hatred in East Germany

INES GEIPEL

Translated by Nick Somers

polity

Originally published in German as *Umkämpfte Zone: Mein Bruder, der Osten und der Hass* © 2019 Klett-Cotta - J.G. Cotta'sche Buchhandlung Nachfolger GmbH, gegr. 1659, Stuttgart

This English translation © Polity Press, 2024

The translation of this book was supported by a grant from the Goethe-Institut.

GOETHE INSTITUT

Polity Press
65 Bridge Street
Cambridge CB2 1UR, UK

Polity Press
111 River Street
Hoboken, NJ 07030, USA

ISBN-13: 978-1-5095-5997-8 – hardback

A catalogue record for this book is available from the British Library.

Library of Congress Control Number: 2023950626

Typeset in 11 on 14pt Warnock Pro
by Cheshire Typesetting Ltd, Cuddington, Cheshire
Printed and bound in Great Britain by CPI Group (UK) Ltd, Croydon

For further information on Polity, visit our website:
politybooks.com

Contents

Acknowledgements

I thank Tom Krausheer for the initial discussion we shared about the book.

Eva-Maria Otte for reading the first version, and for her generosity and support.

Andreas Petersen for his love and our ongoing conversations.

Christine Treml for her calmness and guidance through the text.

Jochen Staadt for his highly pertinent ideas about the history of East Germany.

Tobias Voigt for his knowledge of the battlefields without a home.

Gerit Decke for her ideas and friendship.

Katharina Wilts, Verena Knapp and Marion Heck for their perspicacity when launching the German edition.

I.G., December 2018

CRYSTALS

The snow lies thickly on the ground, and it's still snowing hard. I'm standing at the window looking at the sky. At the snow-flakes falling heavily into the gloom. At the way they spin, get tangled with others and merge with them. At the new pattern they form together. My little brother pulls open the door. Another half hour, then it will stop and it'll be cold enough to get going.

I look at Robby standing in front of me, muffled up like an Eskimo, holding a bucket of cold water in one hand and his toboggan in the other. He is six years old, I'm twelve. It's the winter holidays, February 1973. We're waiting for the cold, then we'll rush down the long flight of steps, up the street, ice the run, smooth it out and link up our toboggans. Watch out, here we come! This is our territory, Zwanzigerstrasse, Weisser Hirsch, Dresden.

Later Robby pulls his scarf from his neck and holds it out to me. He's sweating. He's happy. We run up the street again and again. He slips his hand without a word into mine. Vapour comes out of our mouths. The pallid light of the lampposts, the icy clear night, the glistening snow, the crunching of our steps.

But above all, his small, warm hand.

Slow motion

BEING THERE. His right hand. There's not much else my brother can still move. It's 7 December 2017. I'm sitting at his bedside. Palliative ward, St. Joseph-Stift, Dresden. Robby has a glioblastoma, stage 4. The Herrndorf tumour,[1] he says in greeting. The first operation in April, recurrence in the summer, the second operation at the end of November, a blood clot in the head, then three days ago a stroke. Doesn't look great, he says. No luck. It's good of you to come.

An afternoon. And Robby, who wants to reminisce. For six hours. Is that a lot? I mean, is that a lot of time? He grasps my hand, pulls it to him, places it on his chest. That's where he wants it to be.

Can you see me? he asks softly.

Yes, why?

Because I see two of you. The tumour. It's pushing my eyes apart. Hey, I have to tell you something.

I look at his face: the huge scar on his right temple, the sallow skin, his lips. How words keep emerging between them.

---

[1] Wolfgang Herrndorf was a German author who was diagnosed with the same glioblastoma and committed suicide at the age of forty-eight.

Fast, slow, soft, hesitant. I don't understand anything. As if I had been knocked down by a large animal, as if someone had stuck an ice pick in my brain. Robby, what's going on? What happened? Why didn't you call me? Why so late? Why only . . .? There are so many questions. I don't ask him anything, just stare at his mouth. At the words coming out of them. Like silverfish, I think to myself. Diving, slipping away, wanting to get away, into the darkness.

We were poppers, he says and looks out of the window. Do you know what that is?

I don't think so.

I was eighteen and wore a white suit. I had it made specially. Really cool. We would travel around the villages and go to the discos to pick up girls. My pals and I.

What's a popper?

Not a blueser.

So no Jesus boots.

Right. No long hair, no scruffy clothes, no peace signs, but shaved necks, blow-dried hair, blond streaks, you know, all that flashy gear, and our music.

What kind of music?

The Cure, Prince, Michael Jackson.

Prince, in the mid-1980s in East Germany?

Sure, why not?

And what do poppers do?

Hang out, listen to music, have fun.

Robby shivers a little. Perhaps he has a fever. There must have been a mistake, I think to myself. Something has gone wrong, it can't be right, it's not true. Someone will come along any moment now to fix it. Sorry, they'll say, it's nothing, a data flash, wires crossed, we'll soon put it right. I look towards the door. No one there. What's going on here? Whose idea was this? What's my brother doing in this bed? It's OK, he reassures me and squeezes my hand as if it were a plastic duck. With all the Christmas balls around him, the stars, the hearts, the long string of lights behind his head.

It's supposed to be a reminder of home, Oberlausitz, he nods. Do you remember the Herrnhuter?[2]

Hey, I can't do this just now.

The idea was to comfort children whose parents had gone abroad and sent them to boarding school. The light tells those at home: we're coming to fetch you. Just a little longer, it'll be all right.

Has mother been here?

I don't know. Have you brought any raspberries?

Raspberries?

Yes, fresh ones. They're good for cancer.

How quiet the afternoon is. How easy the world still was yesterday. How naïve, unsuspecting, completely normal. I lay my head on Robby's chest. If only it could stay there quietly for a while until the world finds its way again, until everything gets back to normal.

Is that OK? I ask.

Yes, it's good.

Are you in pain?

No, nothing. I've got more chemicals in me than blood.

Hungry?

They'll be along in a minute. Hey, tell me.

Yes.

What if the journey goes in the other direction? It'll be pretty terrible.

Yes.

I'm scared.

Yes.

Scared of losing consciousness. Will you be here?

I'm here and I'll stay here.

---

[2] Christmas decoration, also known as a Moravian Christmas star.

I put my head back in the place where everything is still normal. As long as it's on Robby's chest, nothing can happen. Do I really believe that? If so, why this feeling? The ice pick in my head is pressing, pushing, it wants to go further. What does it want? Outside it's getting dark. As if the afternoon were a time capsule: floating, far from everything. Just the two of us. Just a brother and a sister. Just Robby and I. But what's happening here? That there were so many other scenarios, just not this one, I think to myself. That being here is completely unreal, surreal. And what's it like for him? Is there a moment of realization? When you have the courage to say to yourself that the journey has begun to go in the other direction? Does it come on a particular day, at a particular hour, at a particular moment? And if so, what next?

CONTINENTAL DRIFT. How small the words are suddenly. As if they wanted to withdraw, shrink, roll up, a bit like rubber bands. No voices around us, no footsteps, no doors closing.

Do you remember? asks Robby, breaking the silence.

What?

When you called me and arranged to meet the next day at the main railway station in Dresden. Come tomorrow to the night train to Budapest, platform 10, you said and then hung up. The next day was 31 August 1989. I remember the date. I'll never forget it. We were standing on the platform. You hardly said a word. You wanted to get away.

I had to.

You wanted to get away, and I thought: How can she do that? Why does she of all people have to go to the West? To a place where we won't exist anymore?

I had to.

You gave me the key to your apartment. The train guard was getting impatient.

The compartment door banged shut. You stood there, alone on the platform, and you didn't wave. Not once.

Take care, sister, you said. And then you followed the train on your moped, through the night. At least that's what you said.

As far as the border, Bad Schandau. I had to.

Robby looks at the ceiling. We are silent. After a while, he says: it's like being in the eye of the hurricane.

What do you mean?

All summer I've been digitizing photos. Our childhood, the Weisser Hirsch, the zinc bathtubs, the Luisenhof. Every night in my mind I get on the train and travel to another time. University, the trips away, the family, the children.

He has thousands of pictures in his head, I think to myself. He's gone through them all again. He's taken his leave.

Don't you want to know what I discovered on the photos? he insists. We grin at each other. Time for Robby's favourite stories. My brother has a weakness for losers, or more precisely for himself as a loser. It's his pet subject. How, shortly after the Wall fell, he and his friends planned to cycle from Dresden to Scotland, and how, on the very first day, he found himself under a motorway bridge in a violent thunderstorm, abandoned by the others, his ID card gone, leaving him no choice but to cycle back. How he returned to the Weisser Hirsch on leave from the army and no longer had a home. Just a note on the door telling him to go to our grandmother's, who had a sofa. How on the first night on the sofa hundreds of moths fluttered around him, and how he fled headlong the next morning to a squat in Dresden-Neustadt.

Stories I know. Pictures that hide other pictures. Robby laughs out loud. His eyeballs pop out. His right hand starts to paddle, as if it were trying to explain his bulging eyes. I would love to hear what he saw on the photos he spent all summer looking at. But my brother is an expert at talking through images. He doesn't like speaking directly. Keep the balls in the air, otherwise you get bogged down. Why does he say that so often?

You have to keep the balls in the air, Robby says like a voiceover, otherwise you'll get trapped.

What do you mean?

It's OK, he says dismissively, later perhaps. Can you massage my hand? That's my Nazi hand.

What?

Don't talk, just massage.

Is that OK?

No, harder. It's a weird feeling when your body just starts to shut down.

I swallow. As a child I used to be able to force back the tears. Stare at the ground and pretend outwardly that I was somewhere else. It used to work quite well. But here?

The story about the moths, I say.

Hm.

How did it go exactly?

You know how it went. Tell me something nice instead.

Raindrops on the windowpane. Fine rivulets disappearing into nothing. Something nice, Robby demands. And if he doesn't have a right to it, who does? He pulls his right hand back and stretches his arm in the air.

What are you doing?

I have to go.

Where?

Leave me. I have to go. I have to go to war.

DIFFERENCES. My brother's hand drops down hard onto the blanket. His gaze drifts to the window. The ice pick again, the pressure in my head, the feeling of slipping away. Where to? Into the world before the loss? To where it all lies ahead? Is that what we tell ourselves? And what then? My brother summoned me when he knew that he had nothing left to lose. When he was sure that we could no longer find any answers. The words feel right, but they have no meaning. They disappear before they're even here.

Don't think about it, says Robby, without moving. There's no point, it doesn't help anyone.

His hand grabs at the empty space. He is perspiring. Rivulets of sweat around his eyes. Slow, gentle threads. His breathing rattles. In the background a machine beeps monotonously. Why is he so quick? I ask myself. How come he always knows?

You seem a bit weighed down, as if you were in slow motion, he says and looks at me out of the corner of his eye.

It's not so easy here.

You can say that again!

Why did we lose sight of each other for such a long time? I retort.

How long?

Five years.

I don't know.

About the moths, he says almost as an aside, it's quite simple: it was at the start of my military service, at the end of October 1985. My first home leave. I was excited because I'd met Emma a week before I was called up.

The Brazilian with the wild hair?

Yes, her. I arrived on a Friday evening with all my kit at our parents' place in Weisser Hirsch. I rang the bell but there was no one there. My key didn't fit. Our name had been removed from the doorplate. It was still my home. It was only then that I saw the note stuck to the door. It was in father's handwriting and said I should go to grandmother's. No explanation. I travelled to town and ended up on the moth-ridden sofa. I didn't see Emma. You know the rest. That's all there is to it.

That's not true. He knows it, I know it. But if I were to ask any more questions, I would be invading my brother's private realm. I don't want to do that. That's not right. It's not the moment. It was never the right moment, something in me echoes. Words, just words, that inevitably end up going nowhere. But what would be the point? Who wants to do that now? It's clear that Robby wants to have a different story in his head from me. Not that there's anything unusual about that. It's just that that our stories are not just variants but *really* different. So different that the disparity cannot be simply ignored. The ice pick in my head has started up again. It clearly wants to pick its way right through to the other side. My brain feels as if it has been skewered and it's icy, as if it were made of metal. The pressure gets more intense. But don't worry, against my better judgement I'll keep it to myself, the story that my brother doesn't tell, can't tell, blocks out. It is the story of an escape, our parents' escape from their earlier life. A life in which my father, according to his 800-page file, was trained from 1973 by the state security service as a 'terror agent', as it was called in the technical jargon. He completed combat training, learned on a dummy how to deliver a knockout blow, and for twelve years travelled under eight different names to the 'enemy territory', the West, not simply as a Stasi informer but as a special agent.

At the end of 1984, father's partisan service was suddenly over. The secret service had no further use for him. In my version of the story, Robby came back at the end of October 1985 to find himself locked out of our parents' house. He wanted to change his military uniform for his white popper suit to go and meet his girlfriend. But he couldn't get in. Our parents had kicked him out. They had left my brother behind and forgotten him. Why? Shortly before, my father had had a final meeting with the Stasi, which according to his file lasted two and a half hours and had only two agenda items: he was released from duty and was to receive some kind of settlement. It was a 'housing exchange' from the rented apartment in Weisser Hirsch, our childhood home, to a house with a garden in Saxon Switzerland. For some reason the deal had to be completed quickly, so my parents' move was more like a moonlight flit. There was not even time to inform their own son of the new home, not to mention what his father had actually been doing for the previous twelve years.

QUESTIONING. Robby moans softly. He is restless. We look at one another as we will never do again. He cannot have known anything of the moth story in my head.

Will you write about it? he asks.

No. No family. I don't want to. I've already said everything there was to say, and what I felt was right. I'm done with it.

Not true.

What's missing?

A lot. Me, above all.

A questioning pause, in which Robby's iPhone rings. It remains on the bed cover. We say nothing. My brother rubs his neck.

What were you saying? he asks.

No, Robby, it's your story. You have to tell it yourself.

You can see how I am. I don't have time for that anymore.

Please no, not that. I can't do it.

Tiny admiral

NO PICTURES. Behind the body the idea. But which one? Four days after our afternoon in the palliative ward, Robby is attached to an intravenous portal system. He can't swallow anymore, he explains on the phone. The next day he comes home. The doctors are strongly against it, but he insists. I sit at his bedside as often as I can. There are no unknowns anymore. The signs are clear. But he is the same old Robby. And he's there. I wonder how the two things can exist in parallel: what was always there, and what has gone forever. My brother is lying in the living room. He can see the Christmas tree, behind it the balcony, the rain on the window, the bare trees on the street. To the right of his bed is the large bookcase.

Most of the time he sleeps, dozes, sinks into a coma. 12 December, 14 December, 17 December. Afternoons, when the silence is there only to ask questions. No sign from him for hours on end. Just his lonely body, the room, the ice pick in my head, which, unusually, has stopped tapping. At some point Robby wakes up, blinks at me, and asks dry-mouthed: did you bring any raspberries? Five punnets, hand-picked from KaDeWe. No reaction from him. He can't eat any more. He can't eat at all.

I have almost no pictures left in me, he says. And instead? – I don't know. Lots of white. A large void. The sudden need to protect him, to take him away, to bring him to a place where everything will be good for him. The sudden need to take a photo, to capture my brother, to resist the significance of the moment. How can it be that every pore in our body is against something, and yet it happens nevertheless? There's no point, says Robby. The ice pick makes itself felt again. May I? I ask and take my iPhone out of my bag. He looks at me steadily for a long time.

I still have *Camera Lucida* you gave me, he says.

Yes.

It was good after all that you went to the West. I got your books and the other things you left behind. Roland Barthes and the lost mother. Those things.

Camera Lucida. The book I carried round with me all the time in my parka pocket at the end of my studies. I don't remember anything about it anymore, except that in some arcane way it was a guiding light for him and that the book spoke ceaselessly of aura, magic, light and that Barthes did not seek solace. He didn't want any. The mother was to remain the lodestar; nothing could compare with her. Barthes looked constantly at photos. He scanned every detail in his mind. But inside of him time didn't exist.

Robby has dozed off. I take his hand and try to speak, to speak to him. Maybe he can hear me. Start, with something, quietly, anything. With the burning leaves in the garden of our childhood, with the unsuccessful search for Easter eggs, the aroma of chestnuts in the pan. I try to find pictures with both of us in them, pictures that define us. Pictures that are not so much about memory but about finding words that make links, that create something, that suspend the tense waiting for one another that perhaps only I feel.

MARKERS. Robby died on 6 January 2018. We had just one month to take our leave of one another. Thirty days. That's all. As long as he was lying in his room in Dresden, I knew what to do. I got into the car and drove to him. Sometimes there was snow on the trees on the motorway, sometimes I looked at the grey winter sky, sometimes it rained, sometimes there were traffic jams. Once I heard a piece on the radio about the desert and how to find one's way there. You should ask Bedouins, it said, and learn to read the signs. Particular markers, watering holes, camel skeletons, withered tree stumps. Wrecked cars or old tyres could also point to the right direction. In the previous four weeks I had seen no markers and also had no idea where I was. But I still managed to get to where I was meant to be, with my brother.

On 6 January 2018 it drizzles. Mild, hazy, slippery. I drive to Dresden to take leave of my brother. He is lying in his bed and looks good, young, relieved, almost disembodied. His lips are open as if he had wanted to ask something before he went. During the weeks I spent at his bedside, it was as if time had lost direction. I just sat there and looked at his face. Sometimes I said a few words. At some point he opened his eyes and said: As a child there was always this thing with my ears. Or: Our ships aren't moving anymore. Or: Feathers, I want feathers. Or: In the Stasi house it's always raining. I imagined an orchestra in the pit but without the energy to start playing. Just a sound now and then, a messy phrase, a couple of loose ends. And yet I never had the feeling that Robby's words were incoherent. I even thought I could make out the pattern. But it was his final chord. Shouldn't it remain unfinished?

REPRESSED LONGING. When I arrived home at night after my visits to Dresden, I sat in front of the computer and googled. Was there really no cure for him? Glioblastoma is the commonest malignant brain tumour. A glioblastoma starts in the white matter. Because of its shape, a glioblastoma is sometimes known as a butterfly tumour. Its growth is diffuse and infiltrating, and a glioblastoma is notable for its inhomogeneous and diverse appearance. A glioblastoma doubles in size every fifty days. A glioblastoma is extremely difficult to treat. The median survival rate of patients with a glioblastoma is 14.6 months. No definitive cure for a glioblastoma has yet been found.

Malignant, inhomogeneous, diffuse, infiltrating, extremely difficult. The only thing I retained was the word butterfly. I saw Robby and myself in our garden as children. My brother had come directly from his biology class and had something on his mind. He showed me the eggs stuck to the old blackthorn bush, the caterpillars in their pupal phase, then the fat admirals perched hungrily on the thistles. On the ground was one that had just slipped out of its chrysalis, all crumpled and trembling. We'll save him, cried Robby, and clapped his hands. I ran off to fetch a bowl of sugared water and dribbled a few drops on it. The tiny admiral cautiously organized its flight apparatus, dipped its proboscis into the water, paused a moment, then flew off and landed with the others.

The butterfly in my brother's head was only nine months old. I sit on his bed and think about the previous four weeks: as if something in me demanded stoically that what Robby had would end up the same way as the tiny admiral. The doctors would surely find the detail that would save him. The unimaginable would not take place. It mustn't, it couldn't, it had to be stopped. What is it? I ask myself. Some kind of madness? A state of shock? An attempt to escape from this feeling of powerlessness? Complete denial? Anxiety corresponds to repressed longing, says Freud, but it's not the same thing. Repression also signifies something. But what?

Robby's hands are cold. How dead people are as soon as they're dead. I count back the days and decide that the previous month was an exception. And what about now? What name do you give to an exception that inevitably becomes the rule? I get up and go over to the large window through which in the final weeks my brother saw his last Advent sky. The Christmas tree on which our childhood decorations hung has been removed. As if something had been preserved in this room, I reflect. In this strange collection of things, to which so many old feelings are attached. I pick up the little Moor, the incense smoker from way back. A leftover from Advent. I'm amazed that it has survived. Perhaps this odd collection represents Robby's wish for coherence, an assurance of a kind, the mark of a time long gone, from now on belonging only to itself.

STEADFAST. How familiar his body is to me. Like my own. Behind the body the idea. But what is there to understand here that was not already there? Everyone is alone in death, writes Canetti. So we are here twice, alone in life and alone in death. Alone twice over. A difficult concept, I find. I remember the first time Robby encountered death. He was maybe five. It was winter. We were by ourselves in the apartment, had made something to eat for ourselves and were sitting at the kitchen table. Suddenly my brother looked at me wide-eyed, jumped up, opened all the doors one after the other, turned on the lights in all the rooms, ran breathlessly through the apartment. He ran and ran until he came back to me and shouted: What is it, death? Is it coming to get me? Where do I go when it's right there in front of me? Will you visit me? How his little body trembled, how frightened he was, how inconsolable.

How to let him go now? Why? What will it be like without you? Sister Rosa from the shift team stands next to Robby's head and asks if I want a coffee. He's breathing, I say, and point to his chest. He's moving. I can still see it. He's alive. He's not dead, it must be a mistake. And everything else is wrong here, too. She nods gently and explains that he has always breathed and that's why he continues to do so. An optical illusion that only goes away after a few hours. How brutal and yet civil death is, I think to myself. It lets Robby continue breathing until everyone around him has got the message. The sky outside the window, the Moravian Christmas lights that just continue to glow, his last washcloth, the little Moor. Perhaps death is a wave. First my brother dies in his bed, then his room, and finally everything on the street.

I look at his face. Is there something that wasn't there before? Something hidden, a mark? I can't see anything. It's all smooth, almost perfectly even. As if the chemistry has also burnt away the years. How young he is. So do we just die like that, as the research seems to think, and the whole thing is nothing but chance, completely arbitrary? Or was there a moment that triggered the crisis in Robby's head? Where could it have started? There are never direct connections, says Ingeborg Bachmann. So there are indirect ones. I can see the tiny admiral, how it weaves around trying to escape from the field of thistles, managing as far as the first lily but then falling back home again. I can see the colours, the stillness, the light at that moment, and my brother, blond, gentle, very delicate.

NEW SCENE. The story of the admiral was our secret. The thing with the sugared water was our secret. That Robby discovered why butterflies avoid shadows was our secret. That grandmother told us how the creatures fluttering around represent souls, and that they help the dead to speak to the living was our secret. My brother was not interested in the soul. He wanted to find out about the business with the shadows. He followed the tiny admiral wherever it went. Later we climbed the steps and he had a panic attack. In my head the butterflies had always been one thing and my brother's panic attack another. They didn't go together, they had nothing to do with one another.

Now, at his bedside, the two scenes mingle and become one. The new scene goes like this: Robby is determined to show me where the tiny admiral sleeps at night. We run home. We're hungry. We sit at the kitchen table. We start to talk about all kinds of things. I tell him grandfather died yesterday. Otto, our mother's father. There is no first moment. Why then am I so sure that this is the beginning?

Our forefathers and their duty

PHANTASMS. Grandfather in a post-war doze in his worn velvet armchair in the living room. His slippers, the grey cardigan, his hands on the armrests, the horn-rimmed glasses, the blank expression. He was there and not there. A silent, shrivelled man with chronic stomach ulcers. Otto Grunert, born 1905 in Meuselwitz, at the time part of Saxony. Undulating wetlands, lignite forests, all kinds of industry: briquette factories, iron foundries, steel mills, machine tools. A town of boiler mechanics, stokers, hand carts and beer drinkers. In winter lots of sulphur-smelling fog, in summer opencast mines flooded and turned into vast bathing lakes. Meuselwitz as the phantasm of the 'colourless desolation', as described later by Wolfgang Hilbig,[1] who never really got the town out of his system.

After the liquidation of his insolvent transport company, however, Otto Grunert left Meuselwitz and moved to Dresden, where he met Elisabeth Horn, who was the same age as him and came from a faded cloth-making dynasty. They married in 1929. Nine months later came the first of eight children. In

---

[1] Novelist and poet, born in Meuselwitz.

1932 grandfather was employed by the German administrative authorities, first in the Saxon Ministry of Finance, later in the Ministry of Internal Affairs. A career that followed strict political lines: district administrative college in Seifersdorf, Gau management school in Augustusburg, a course on racial policy in Dresden.

He joined the Nazi party in March 1933. Then through the block warden ranks – Blockwart, Blockwalter, Blockleiter. Elisabeth Grunert belonged to the National Socialist Women's League. In the photos in the personnel files, grandfather soon has almost no hair left and looks glum. His wife makes a completely different impression: wiry, high-necked dresses, Protestant, determined. She has great ambitions. The inner driving force is money, career, security, upward mobility. In 1937 Otto Grunert volunteered for the military. Four years in barracks in Dresden. Three weeks after the start of the Russian campaign, when personnel were needed for the administration of the huge Reich Ministry for the Occupied Eastern Territories, he applied straightaway to work in the East, took two weeks' leave, organized his departure and travelled to the Nazi 'Ordensburg'[2] Falkenburg am Krössinsee in Pomerania, where he trained for three weeks to be 'put into shape', as Helmut Lethen[3] might say, for what was to come.

What was to come is still described by mother as our happiest years. Seen from outside, it could only be described as a disaster. Am I inside or outside? One or the other, but that's for later. For now, Otto Grunert made his way from Krössinsee to Riga, capital of Latvia. He arrived there on the last day of August 1941. The Germans had occupied the city exactly two months earlier. A huge red flag with black swastika hung from the National Opera. And that's not all. The terror of the

---

[2] Elite Nazi training facility; the name is derived from the medieval Teutonic Order.
[3] Germanist and cultural scholar.

Stalin regime was followed without pause by Hitler: pogroms, mobile commandos, lynchings, thousands dead. It was called the summer executions, controlled by Einsatzgruppe A and carried out for the most part by Latvian auxiliary groups. After the raids in the city, the mass murder moved to the forests of Biķernieki on the road heading north-east from the city.

MOBILITY. The German military requisitioned Riga as a supply base and distribution centre for the northern section of the front. The city was intended as a lifeblood for the war but also as a transhipment and storage centre for Hitler's 'economic expansion'. Above all, it became a European slaughterhouse. When Otto Grunert started working for the Reichskommissariat Ostland in early September 1941, almost 30,000 Riga Jews had been confined to the large ghetto in Maskavas Forštate. Only for two months. In the first massacre at the end of November 1941, 15,000 of them were executed within a few hours in the forest of Rumbula. In the second, eight days later, 12,500 were killed at the same site.

And grandfather? Did he realize where he was? What did he feel about the orgies of extermination taking place close at hand? Was he involved? He never talked about it, there is no personal testimony, and mother defends Riga like a crypt. No explanations reach the outside world. The refusal to speak exists to this day. There are just the files. What strikes me immediately is the business with grandfather's stomach. It started to play up in autumn 1941. A stubborn indigestibility. Or: the story of the bureaucrats of terror and their internal organs. Has anyone ever described what happens to the stomach, heart, lungs and kidneys in an atmosphere of terror? His new position as government secretary responsible for accounts, budget and staff guaranteed mobility, triple the salary, various benefits, promotion at least every two years, a summer villa on the Baltic in Latvia on the sandy beach of Jūrmala, a cook, an official chauffeur-driven car, a nanny, and a large fashionable apartment. All this would have been unthinkable in Dresden. Was that enough, I mean enough compensation, for living in a slaughterhouse?

In April 1942 a brief letter from grandfather to the Reichskommissariat trusteeship: 'I request the following furniture from the ghetto stocks for my official apartment: 1 bed or couch, bedding, table linen, 1 linen cupboard, 4 chairs, 1 sideboard, 2 tables (for children). Heil Hitler!' Request for ghetto stocks for my official apartment. What words. So he knew full well what was going on. At least that much. The letter also indicates that the family was about to arrive in Riga. Why? What would five small children do in such a terrible place? The counterbalance, the refuge from what grandfather approved with his signature every day? The Dresden family arrived by taxi from Tilsit. They drove to the centre of Riga, to Laudonstrasse 4, and stopped in front of a large building with stone cats over the entrance. It was spring in the fourth year of the war. The family was reunited, a German occupying community pretending to live a normal life in the heart of the inferno.

A city where violence was the norm, with thousands of dead, a German milieu, and the horses that shied at the piles of snow on the streets because of the stench of the corpses underneath. In the evening after work, visits from the neighbours in Laudonstrasse 4. Wilhelm Burmeister and his wife, for example. Burmeister, head of the Political and Administration Department in the Reichskommissariat Ostland and deputy of Reichskommissar Hinrich Lohse. Burmeister, who travelled specially from Riga to the Ministry of Justice in Berlin because he needed to know whether he risked criminal charges following his service in the East. No risk, the Ministry assured him. What was happening in the East were 'merely events of metalegal character'. So no reason to be concerned.

Did this reassurance also provide comfort when the family dined together in the evening? Probably not. If so, it was not enough to relieve grandfather. In late summer 1942, his doctor reported an extremely 'poor general state of health and chronic insomnia'. He recommended 'urgent leave in the Reich so as to restore the ability to work'. There was no leave, and his condition failed to improve. Whatever. Instead, there were the agreed promotions: in July 1942 to Landesinspektor, in June 1944 to Landesoberinspektor. What did a Landesoberinspektor do in the terror of occupied Riga? The file contains an affidavit by him from late October 1943: 'I have been instructed today of my duty to confidentiality, also regarding measures by the administration and military units and other incidents known to me outside of my work.'

What could that mean? All of the Jews in Riga had disappeared and been exterminated, most of the huge ghetto in Maskavas Forštate, with thousands of Jews from all over Europe, had been transferred to Kaiserwald concentration camp, as Heinrich Himmler pointed out in early October 1943 in his monstrous speech in Poznań: 'The Jewish question in the territories occupied by us will be solved by the end of this year.' Not extinction, but total extinction. Transports, work commandos, marching columns, special measures, the statistical horror of the camps. An endless series of dark pictures goes through my mind and disappears directly into the abyss. It would be an understatement to say that I can't imagine it. I just can't. Almost none of the 25,000 German Jews survived Riga.

I want to get the words for this right. Words that know what they are saying, that support each other, that do not absorb or cushion anything but that inform. But what words are there for that? And what does 'right' mean? The stream that doesn't stop. The ground that slips away. It is also a stream through time. There's no point in running away from it. I can see grandfather in his post-war armchair. Lifting my brother onto his lap. Holding Robby's little body away from him. The two looking at one another and not appearing too happy. And there's a girl – me, with a military-style cut and itchy woollen stockings – observing the scene. My brother is three, he's struggling, he wants to get away, to be put down *now*, immediately. He never wanted to go to this man. Is that what Robby meant in the palliative ward? When he said: write about it? Am I supposed to say what he didn't like and was never able to touch or look at?

INEVITABLE. The disaster that was now entering the fifth year of war. The Red Army, which started its major offensive on Berlin, and Hitler, who now functioned only by autosuggestion. Special commando 1005, which started to exhume and burn thousands of corpses from the Baltic massacres. Laudonstrasse 4, where the eighth Grunert child was born, and grandfather, whose stomach was on strike. There's more: his personnel file now reads like a series of sick leave notes. The nervous system had long gained the upper hand. 'Sick and unfit for work' was written on the notes that grandmother sent habitually to the central department. The maelstrom of collapse had begun to gnaw at bodies. Its pull became stronger every day. No one and nothing was safe anymore.

The downfall in the summer of 1944 and the slaughterhouse of Riga, that had long become a trap for the occupiers as well. Grandmother and four of her children managed to board a ship for Hamburg in early July. The two oldest children were put in a home near Danzig. Grandfather was transferred in August to SS-Battalion Schatz. The unit was part of the anti-partisan campaign, the last desperate ad hoc units raging against 'irregular enemies' in the dead zone between the Red Army and the Wehrmacht. War as work, war as duty. The killing had found its way into families and turned everything into the front. The chaos was everywhere.

The files show that in August 1944 grandfather was at the Seelager SS military training area at the northern tip of Courland. And a request by his wife in October 1944 to Alfred Rosenberg, Reich Minister for the Occupied Eastern

Territories. A rescue bid. Grandmother writes that her 'husband has been serving since 15 September in a new unit' and requests: 'I'm sure my husband can also serve further away from the front line.' The reason: 'As the father of healthy thriving children, he is still urgently needed as a parent.' The letter ends with the postscript: 'I myself also served in the war in Riga as head of the ward for wounded soldiers in war hospital 2/608. I was awarded the Gold Cross of Honour of German Mothers in June 1944.'

Why do I need to know all these details? What am I looking for? For a grandfather who would say at some point: that's it, done, over? For a grandmother who would manage just once to utter an honest sentence about the time in Riga? It didn't happen. I know that. So what then? At the end of November 1944, SS-Unterscharführer Grunert was to be posted to Libau (Liepāja) in the Courland cauldron. So he didn't manage to get away from the unit. Return cancelled, it says on the order. But grandfather will survive. That's easy to say today. At the end of 1944, no one knew what would happen. At the end of 1944, there was a fierce argument about who was responsible for him, and there were all kinds of special movement orders – to Libau, to Danzig, to a satellite camp of Dachau concentration camp. In mid-January 1945 another radio message: 'Grunert to be posted to Libau'.

Grabbing hold of a lifeline to escape. The woman who puts away her husband's service revolver and doesn't shoot herself because she wants to know what life is. The soldiers who jump onto the last ship before Hel and break their oath because it has no meaning anymore. That was another way of escaping. So what am I looking for? For some kind of way out of the inevitable? Why? For grandfather? Unlikely. For Robby? For myself? Otto Grunert was able to survive the last months of the war in the Wehrmacht. On 7 May 1945 the Red Army crossed the Loschwitz Bridge and entered the ruins of Dresden. The war was over.

In July 1945 a questionnaire from the mayor, basically a first round of denazification. Four pages. Head of household, wife, children, servants. And countless questions. 'Where did you live from January 1942 to now?' – 'Until mid-October 1942 in Dresden Bühlau, then on Plauenscher Ring,' wrote grandfather neatly in the old-fashioned Sütterlin script. And Riga? No mention of the years there. Nor any mention of his time in the SS. It never happened.

BEACON

You can't get out of there. Try as you may, rejoices Robby, staring at the sky. What are you talking about? – The black holes up there. It's August 1973. Above us only stars. We are crouched together. In a field. What holes? I ask. There is so much pressure, he beams, that no one can escape. Dust, gases, rays, everything is swallowed up. They are blacker than the universe and devour everything, even light. You're simply not there, you can't be seen. As if you had never existed. As if you were shrouded in a magic cloak. Not bad, eh? – And how do you know that? – Steffen told me. He heard it on the radio from the West.

Robby and I are at the pioneer camp in Saxon Switzerland. During the day I hardly see him. He's with the others in the forest or at the swimming baths, while I work with grandmother in the kitchen. In the evening we meet behind the house on the high field. My brother loves the sky and he loves talking about it. Everything I know about the stars I have from him. The field is quiet and cool. There's the Big Dipper, says Robby admiringly. His little body snuggles up to me and he lays his head on my shoulder while his hand reaches out to the universe. Sagittarius, Cygnus, the Milky Way, he cries. Do you know what a fixed star is? There are three thousand of them up there. But most of them can't be seen. They're too far away, too small, or not hot enough to give off enough light. They remain invisible. – Like the black holes? – No, not at all.

ROYAL RELICS

The Weisser Hirsch, Kurparkstrasse, Villa Waldesruh, the rhododendron fields, the tennis courts, the sound of balls being hit. And just beyond the dull clay the Dresden Heath. The last street names are Am Hochwald and Heideröschen. After them comes the winding sand path, which becomes lighter after every bend, the trees getting closer together, the business of the forest, the cracking and rustling. Robby and I are out walking. We know precisely where we're heading, to the fragment pit. It's quite a long way. Red symbols are carved on the tree bark: a compass, scissors, an anchor, a cow's tail. There are five to pass and then we're there.

My brother takes our trowels out of the bag, heads for the pit, pauses a moment and then points to an area of sand. That's where we start. We poke, scrape and say nothing. It's difficult and dusty work. Stones, wood, bones, slim pickings. Fairly soon I can't be bothered anymore. Then Robby jumps up. Look, he shouts, holding up a lump of something. We examine it. The head of an old porcelain doll. Its left eye is loose. Come on, keep at it, says my brother. Our trophies that evening: a lead seahorse, a chipped jewellery box, a rusty fork and the doll's head. Robby claims that the buried treasures once belonged to the king of Saxony. Who told him that? – Grandmother. She knows about those things.

In a vacuum

OMISSIONS. Riga, the missing section that was cut out and stowed away in the family safe after the war. How often, how many millions of German families were like that? The collapse that shouldn't have happened. But why the missing section? Is that right? Where there's a missing section there should be a hole, a void, an emptiness. There should be no sound there. But the images in my head of post-war East Germany are all about cheering. Parades through streets of rubble, large collectives on huge building sites, crowded rooms at party congresses. The noise must have been deafening. Like a vast mass of people cheering loudly. Flags, pennants, torches, banners, flushed, guileless faces. The better Germany, a new party, with its own state and religion for a red future. Playing at deliverance, relief, victory, or what exactly?

I try to turn down the sound a bit. Perhaps something will emerge. Will something else appear from under all this obsessive boosting? The years of the great sigh of relief, the reconstruction, the digging of new foundations. But wasn't it legitimate to hope? After the disaster, wasn't this just what was needed – a huge sea of enthusiasm? All of those happy-looking faces. I stare at the portraits of Stalin, the huge fluttering flags, the slogans: 'The dreams of the Communists are dreams for reality.' Was that ecstasy or hypnosis? And what would be the difference? The degree of promise or denial? The soundless images rapidly start to turn sour. They appear to be getting ragged. The exaggerated claims fade out and are replaced directly by a different reality. 'With all its troubling aspects, the post-war period inflicted immense damage,' wrote the author Susanne Kerckhoff in 1948 in *Berliner Briefe*. 'We were all looking forward too much to the end of the war and the victory of freedom. We weren't emotionally prepared because we wanted above all to escape from the cage and get rid of the criminals.'

In summer 1949, the Jewish philosopher Hannah Arendt also returned to Germany for the first time. In *Besuch in Deutschland* she wrote in astonishment about the ruined capital: 'The Berliners are the only ones taking the trouble to identify the similarities between Hitler and Stalin.' And she observed that the 'police regime in the eastern zone is this time almost unanimously detested by the inhabitants' and 'an even more pronounced atmosphere of camaraderie, secrecy, insinuations and posturing exists there than in the Nazi period'.

But what was the situation really like? What did the post-fascist reality in the east of Germany feel like? What kind of society was being created there? What was happening with the victims, perpetrators, followers and onlookers? Who had the political say at the outset? The makeshift solutions, the war wound, the hunger. The Nazis, the anti-Nazis, the resistance, the concentration camp survivors, the refugees, Wehrmacht returnees, new arrests. The bombed-out inhabitants, those buried under the rubble, the missing persons, those condemned to live. A period of upheaval – or rather of turning inside out – a time of crisis, of raw nerves. The Communist paradise looked more like a battered shredder cosmos. But how could it have been otherwise? In West Germany, Arendt wrote, the guilt was being manically swept away, and in the

East? The dead and the enthusiasm. With all the appearance of two sides of a lost, broken world. I have started jotting notes to myself. There is no other way. Notes that point to the missing section that was not allowed to exist, that was being energetically rewritten. As what?

HINTERLANDS. The Rose restaurant in East Berlin and the Ulbricht group, who returned to Germany from Moscow at the end of April 1945 to play out in the microcosm of the capital the plans for how the country should be after Hitler: 'It must look democratic, but we need to have control of everything.' A sentence by Ulbricht turned into a document of its time by Wolfgang Leonhard in *Die Revolution entlässt ihre Kinder*. What came next can now be comfortably recounted as history. The files have been dug up, the archives broken open. But does that help? Are we any the wiser? Do we know how much material was destroyed or was kept, stored away in a safe place? A complicated matter. A complicated time as well. Hard, confused, delicate, fragile.

This thing with the notes. On the first one is Walter Ulbricht, later responsible for the Wall. It's impossible to recount his story in full, despite the fact that he pushed his way to the centre of the political stage in East Germany and was the central figure until 1971. A quarter-century of total power. What kind of hinterland was there to give him this power? Where and by whom was this new dictator made? The German Communists who emigrated to the Soviet Union after 1933, Stalin's Great Purge in 1937/38 and the Gulag system. The number of Germans murdered was devastating. In April 1938, 70 per cent of the nearly 5,000 German Communists in Soviet exile were arrested. Forty-one of the sixty-eight top Politburo and Central Committee members were murdered. A good two hundred political cadres who had survived Stalin's Great Purge returned to Germany from Moscow directly after the war. Deeply scarred but relieved to have escaped the gloom.

Among them just two top Party officials: Wilhelm Pieck and Walter Ulbricht.

These two knew about everyone's fate; they could be put under pressure by Stalin and for that very reason were chosen as the inner power nexus in the new state. They observed their Communist oath of silence and sang the praises of the Soviet Union. Two individuals who knew precisely about those who had survived – when, how and under what conditions – and those whom Stalin had had murdered. They also knew who had been kept in the Gulags until Adenauer's trip to Moscow in September 1955 so that the new success story in East Germany could be celebrated and not marred by terrible accounts of suffering. Who were they? How did they live with this knowledge?

HIDING PLACES. The beginnings in East Germany were fraught with danger. The blond little girl with the short-cropped hair, me, was not yet there. I didn't exist. Despite this, just a word, a photo, a smell or the sound of a voice is enough to conjure up the flavour of the time. A world of soot and ashes, a huge ruined landscape, an allegory inside me. What is it saying to me? We are told quite firmly today that we are just physical matter, cells and energy, but it tells me that this can't be the case. Our pores also remember things we have not and could not have experienced. They are souls, repositories of sensations in which an unknown time can creep in at will. I'm thinking of Robby. Who else? Of the primordial cell, the nucleus. It's not here. I miss it. I ask myself why we never spoke about all this and could never do so. About where we come from, who we are.

About grandfather, for example, and his first summer after the war. The Grunerts had given up the apartment in Bühlau. The people knew about him there and about his time in Riga. They moved with four children to his mother-in-law in the middle-class Plauenscher Ring, which had not suffered as badly from the bombing. Grandfather was unable to find a proper job. For a time he worked somehow, repairing vehicles in a garage in Übigau. But how was he really getting on? Was he happy to have survived? He was most certainly afraid. The fear came in phases, depending on where and when arrests took place. There were lots of rumours. The denazification in the first months after the war was spontaneous and random. No one was safe. A neighbour's denunciation could be enough for internment in an NKVD camp or for being taken away by the Russians.

Directive 24, designed to standardize the procedure, only came into effect in January 1946. Grandfather's fear, which became more telling than his silence. He became dangerously ill, so ill that he needed several operations on his stomach. But the interventions provided little relief. The serious inability to digest anything remained. This was one of the reasons that prompted my grandparents to move with their children to Bad Gottleuba. There they managed a trade union holiday home in the forest. A photo shows them standing on the wide steps in front of the new house. Thin, with solemn post-war expressions. Tall spruce trees surrounding the property. It looked like a hiding place, and that's what it was.

I have no idea how my grandparents viewed the new society in which they were now living. Where the pictures of Riga were that they must still have had in their heads. In their backwater they probably didn't have much idea about what was going on in the country. It was a time of personal questionnaires, doctored certificates, denunciations and reinvention. A time of gambling with the truth and rewriting biographies. The denazification process in East Germany came to an end in March 1948. Six months later my grandparents returned to Dresden. Otto Grunert started working in an engineering factory, and his wife became head of a Konsum sales outlet. They moved to an apartment on Fetscherplatz. Grandfather sat in his armchair in the living room. Sometimes he rubbed his stomach because it hurt so much.

The GDR was founded in October 1949. One of the first official measures was a law waiving sanctions and granting civil rights to former members and supporters of the Nazi party and officers in the fascist Wehrmacht. Nazi activists and war criminals who had escaped persecution by giving false information about themselves, by fleeing or by other means were excluded from this moratorium. It is not clear how grandfather understood this law in his case. How could he know that proceedings for crimes in the 'Eastern territories' would be cancelled in practically all cases? Even more, the General Commissariat, particularly its non-military members, started to gain a reputation for actually having *resisted* the regime towards the end.

IMMINENT DANGER. A series of fierce political battles took place after the war between the Ulbricht group, the Communists who returned from the concentration camps, the emigrants coming back from the West and those Communists who had remained in the country under Hitler – a Communist cadre trained in conspiracy and solidarity. They were fighting about power in the new country and about who would reform and rebuild East Germany and in which direction. Denazification, expropriation, collectivization, the new elite was used merely as a testing ground rather than as a serious attempt to deal with the situation. They took decisive action: in August 1949 the amnesty for NSDAP (Nazi Party) members, in October 1949 the investigation of newspapers and magazines and the first prohibitions, just days later the incorporation of the judiciary into the state administration, then the screening of public officials who had emigrated or been held prisoner in the West. Ulbricht won the skirmishes and gained the upper hand. In fact, that's not quite true. There weren't any options or negotiations in the first place. There was Stalin in Moscow. He made all the decisions on his own.

This thing with the notes. The first note: Ulbricht and his diverse initiative groups who ensured 'order' in the country.

The second note: Buchenwald as the original anti-fascist base. A word that automatically sets off powerful ripples. It's quite a story. Buchenwald, which would shove its way into the family archives of East Germany. Buchenwald, the state myth, the site where East Germany was founded and the basis for its collective identity forged. There should be lots of notes for this place. Buchenwald was originally one of the largest concentration camps on German soil, where almost 266,000 people were interned between 1937 and April 1945. In no other concentration camp was the Communist resistance organized so 'unusually effectively' as on Ettersberg Hill near Weimar. From 1942, the depot, the labour office and the hospital were controlled by red inmate trustees. They held key positions in a captive community with the power of life and death: of the 56,000 inmates who died in Buchenwald, 72 were German Communists. When the camp was liberated, the US secret service members were frustrated to find themselves confronted by a select group of German Communists looking like 'wealthy businessmen' and 'self-appointed aristocrats'.

Seventy-two out of fifty-six thousand? Is that possible? My eyes look in disbelief at the two figures. How can this come about? I go back in time. I see a fourteen-year-old girl with short-cropped hair blundering over the huge site. It is 1974 and the obligatory visit to Buchenwald. In an hour we will assemble in the roll-call area and take the oath making us citizens of the GDR. It will be about allegiance, struggle, revolution and ideals, about our role as 'true patriots'. The pictures in the camp documentary, the coming-of-age oath,[1] the forlorn grey assembly between the SS barracks, shivering together. An act without opposition. Seven years later it was Robby's turn. What did he think of it? Did he shiver with cold as we had?

[1] *Jugendweiheschwur* – an oath taken by adolescents in the GDR pledging loyalty to the state.

Buchenwald. The wall, the block which separated good and evil. Those who are not with us are against us, as they said. Buchenwald and its damaged, tortured bodies, which we young people taking the oath understood without knowing the reason. Why did I keep going back there later? What was I looking for? What bothered me about this place? The camp? The massive rewriting? Which I couldn't have known anything about? Which no one except the inner party circle knew about? In fact, for all its merit, including the evacuation in the last days of the camp, saving the lives of tens of thousands of Jews, when Buchenwald was liberated, the Communist camp network came under acute suspicion of having been actively complicit in the Nazi crimes. The imputations were serious, referring to the criminal offence of murder as a systemic disciplinary principle within the camp, and to self-interest and lust for power. The first Allied concentration camp dossier, published on 24 April 1945, noted in consternation how the inmates themselves organized a murderous regime within the Nazi terror. The US authorities therefore searched not only for SS camp guards but also for German Communists who were to be charged with crimes against humanity. A core group was held for weeks for investigation on the site of the camp after it had been liberated. Some of them were arrested.

I remember early 1994 and the media fuss at *Geheimakte Buchenwald* and the book *Der gesäuberte Antifaschismus* appearing six months later to give some order to the sensational documents. I read every single document and recall my reaction. It was all wrong. What had we been told all this time about East Germany? What did it all mean? The GDR – politically a state on standby, officially a country of campaigns and pictures of cheering crowds, internally a rickety structure close to collapse made up of victims, perpetrators and followers. Dominated from the outset by a group of trained political cadres, who fought bitterly for power and boldly

rewrote their own histories. What hope was there? It was clear
that this revelation of the murderous camp activities would
have completely compromised the 'Communist fighting fel-
lowship'. The Moscow returnees led by Ulbricht also had to
face up to these revelations. It would not have been possible
to explain to the sceptical and disheartened inhabitants of East
Germany and the rest of the world that the better Germany
had been launched by murderers, even if they had been
fighting for their survival as camp inmates under extreme conditions of captivity. This information was volatile, an imminent
danger.

ROOF RABBITS. The Gordian Knot of the post-war period
and the tangled thicket of its endless stories. Grandfather
sitting motionless in his armchair. The hoped-for radical
change, which soon turned out to be something else. It was
the marauding and murdering Soviets, who roamed the land
not as liberators but as conquerors and subjugated the East
German people. It was the forced merger of the Communists
and Social Democrats in April 1946, after which 20,000 Social
Democrats lost their jobs, 100,000 fled to the West, 5,000 were
interned in camps, and 400 were murdered. It was the special
policy of the new party towards the Nazis, which basically said:
'If you follow the party line, we won't remind you of your past,
although we know about it.' Initially, 80 per cent of the teachers in East Germany were former members of the NSDAP,
45 per cent of the doctors, and around three-quarters of the
university medical researchers, as Henry Leide pointed out in
his book *NS-Verbrecher und Staatssicherheit.*

Realities that shouldn't have been allowed, an East Germany
that became a battlefield and real test: buffeted, disillusioned,
makeshift. The biting winters, the food rationing. Two American
cigarettes or 44 reichsmarks for a loaf of rye bread. Most of the
recently reopened schools had to shut again because of the
shortage of coal. People met in heated rooms for the homeless,

in soup kitchens or on the black market. There were soon no cats and dogs in Berlin anymore, because these 'roof rabbits', as they were called, were being served in place of rabbit. SED party officials, Nazis, gold diggers, criminals, women and lots of young people squatted separately at tables in the canteens on the country's huge construction sites and furtively observed one another. Every table had its own truth, its own unspoken secrets. How to make the people of East Germany accept the new world when the Communists couldn't even get their own story straight?

Penury in the country, a ruthless and clandestine change of scenery in the new party. Three-quarters German Buchenwald Communists against one-quarter Moscow returnees. That ought to have been enough. But Pieck and Ulbricht had a set of highly incriminating notes on the former Buchenwald inmates, also documented in *Der gesäuberte Antifaschismus*. They knew not only about the Gulags and the relatives interned there but also about the Buchenwald complex. 'Most of the German comrades did not behave well there,' it said. Or: 'Thugs, hangman's assistants, 20 beaten to death'. There were internal hearings. The testimonies were unequivocal. The witnesses reported credibly about the systematic use of injections in the camp, about the 'injection squad' and the 'lethal injections', in other words injections with phenol, air or germs. And then, in autumn 1946, the investigation within the party, at which nineteen former Buchenwald inmates were forced to testify. The result: the accusations were refuted almost without exception and the 'outstanding service' of the accused in the camp confirmed. Despite the clear evidence, the commission, along with Pieck and Ulbricht, buried their dark knowledge of Buchenwald. Why? This coup put an end to the fierce factional infighting between the Moscow group and the initially so self-assured Buchenwald Communists. They were in the hands of the party leadership, vulnerable to blackmail and easy to manipulate for the new Moscow line.

WHITEWASH. But wasn't panic still the most obvious reaction at this time, the fear of falling into the abyss? Of being unable to deal with the loss and suffering? Was there not the most hopeless fear of collapse? In society but also at the individual level? What would have become of grandfather if he had been capable of facing up to his time in Riga? What did saying nothing mean under these circumstances? Was it an unwritten law that gave the authorities the power to rule an entire country? It is clear that everyone had something different to hide. The Moscow returnees, the Wehrmacht officers, my grandfather, the red Kapos from Buchenwald.

Their past did not disappear. The investigations continued. In 1950 the Soviet military administration weighed in and arrested two top Communist cadres from Buchenwald Ernst Busse, after 1945 Minister of the Interior and deputy chief minister of Thuringia, and Erich Reschke, Thuringia's chief of police and then director of Bautzen prison. They were both carted off to the Gulag on the basis of testimony from fellow inmates. They were never seen again. Meanwhile, the West had also become aware of the embarrassing information about Buchenwald. In early 1947, in the run-up to the Dachau Buchenwald trial, West German newspapers reported on the 'secret of Buchenwald'. Now an open secret, it developed into a political stigma. It was like milk mixing with water. The evil dripped, trickled and spread unhindered.

Once again my Buchenwald visits. Once again the big sky over the plain, the fluffy high clouds and my question as to what I was actually seeking there. Why did I want to go there? On the road from Jena to Erfurt, the Buchenwald bell tower appeared on the hill to the right of the autobahn. A prominent point, an icon that in my head had long begun to lead a dark life of its own. Perhaps our memory in retrospect is also a kind of camp memory that is just trying to escape, to find the one door finally to get out?

The conflict regarding the political stigma of the Buchenwald Communists. The complicity, the guilt that now became a new enemy to be fought just as fiercely as the resistance in the camp. The milk of history had to be stopped. Campaigns were started, commissions and committees formed for that purpose, contacts made throughout the world, survivor associations polarized, and exonerating material obtained to whitewash the Buchenwald narrative. All kinds of activities by which, as the years went by, the situation was even gradually turned around, making it possible in this way to develop a heroic catechism that increasingly glorified the camp history and the Communist resistance. And then at some point the country's children assembled in Buchenwald, freezing, shivering, and pledging their oath.

There can be no doubt about the brutal constraints of the camp. It would also be inhuman and historically extreme to hold it against the German Communists for wanting to rescue themselves from their predicament. But what they made of it is still unacceptable and consequential. There can't have been another place in Germany where Communist and Nazi brutality were so interwoven and then after 1945 so emphatically separated from one another. At all events, Buchenwald was completely unsuited to become the main bastion of Communist resistance and a state myth. But that's precisely what happened.

THE BRICK WALL. The memory cast in concrete over the camp in the 1950s was also part of the Buchenwald complex. Buchenwald was a pivotal element in the necessary pact between the new authorities and the East German people. It had enormous symbolic value. As a consummate expert in the strategic rewriting of history, Moscow needed this site. The key novel *Nackt unter Wölfen* by Bruno Apitz [translated into English as *Naked Under Wolves*] was published in 1958. Written by a former Buchenwald inmate, it described the

dramatic fight by the German Communists to save a Jewish
youth in the camp. The author naturally knew of the accusations and continuing attacks on his comrades-in-arms. He
knew about the degradations and arrests. Apitz wanted to testify about this deadly place, about the fear and survivors' guilt.
He felt compelled to do so. The years in Buchenwald weighed
heavily. He was tormented by his experience there but also by
the repudiation of the memory after the war, particularly by his
party. The draft manuscript shows how the author wanted to
make his novel a testimony to his martyrdom. He needed it as
a lawyer, as a defence of the suffering, as a duty, and as a space
for dealing with it.

In many respects, the witness's status was uncertain. First,
the text was unwanted. When Apitz took it to DEFA[2] in 1954,
he was turned away. A year later, he asked for a loan from the
writers' association in Berlin to be able to write the book. This
was turned down as well. The author was not in good shape at
the time. He had practically no source of income, his marriage
had ended, and his health was affected by the long period of
internment. Only his friends and the Mitteldeutscher Verlag
gave him the strength to continue with his project. The novel
was finally completed in 1957. But what kind of book was it?
Did it dare to reveal any of the narrative that the Communists
had agreed to keep silent about after Buchenwald? Already in
April 1945, the US authorities had been shocked to discover
– as was also documented in *Der gesäuberte Antifaschismus*
– that the German Communists under interrogation all
gave the same stereotypical answers: 'When the army inter-
rogators asked the members of the Communist organization
about their brutality, it was like running up against a brick
wall. "No Communist admitted more than that the criminal elements were roughly dealt with in the struggle for
power".'

---

[2] Deutsche Film-Aktiengesellschaft – GDR state-owned film studio.

How did Apitz shape his written testimony, given that he wanted the novel to be seen explicitly as such but at the same time sought rehabilitation through it? Some of his early descriptions of what really happened in Buchenwald are taken over word for word. The dedication also makes direct reference to what really happened: 'I greet our dead comrades-in-arms of all nations whom we left behind in Buchenwald. In their honour, many of the personages in the book are named after them.'

The author's shifting view of the reality was no doubt one reason for its continued popularity. The first print run of 10,000 copies sold out overnight. Eighteen months later 200,000 copies had already been sold. The book was an international success. There cannot have been many readers who did not derive their idea of Buchenwald from it. But does this not make it even more important to ask just how much of the book is a recollection? How far is the narrator going in his story? Is there a 'brick wall' in the text as well? And if so, what happens in front of and behind it?

The version completed in October 1957 is Apitz's direct reaction to the long-standing suspicion that had dominated the discussion since the end of the war regarding the 'red combat readiness'. He addressed the imputations directly and based the story on the disputed facts. The systematic killing of fellow inmates by lethal injection with the assistance of the German Communists is not glossed over, nor the role of the red inmate functionaries in the life-and-death compilation of the transport lists. Susanne Hantke, who published the revised version of *Nackt unter Wölfen* in 2014 with a view to revealing the author's original manuscript for the first time, surmised quite plausibly: 'Apitz wanted not only to highlight the achievements of political inmate functionaries in resisting but also and above all to put together a narrative that would describe the ambivalent experience of their powerlessness and lack of alternatives in carrying out the work that the SS ordered them to do.'

From the outset, however, this blunted the critical distinction between the captive situation of the inmates and the crimes they committed. It did not refute the discredited acts but rather denied the extent of the murderous activities, the question of complicity in them and of how to address this properly. In the original version, the historical truth went unmentioned, and the underlying reality was hidden behind the 'wall'. Criminal acts were disguised behind a highly emotionalized literary mask. One of the key scenes early in the novel describes the SS camp doctor Papa Berthold administering a lethal injection to a Polish inmate, but not a word is written about the systematic lethal injection policy of the German Communists with regard to their Polish fellow inmates. The scene is therefore ambivalent in terms of responsibility, but the issue of participation in the crimes is placed unreachably behind the wall.

The result was an anachronistic text that revealed and concealed at the same time. The problematic scenes became a cypher hinting at the facts of the extermination in the camp and the major trauma experienced by the German Communists. The knowledgeable reader is thus fully aware, while the uninformed reader is left with the censored memory of Buchenwald. Apitz does not go against the Communist language dictate, but through a system of inferences leaves it to the written testimony within the novel to speak the unspeakable.

And yet, even this multiform rescue attempt by Apitz, itself testimony to the schizophrenic situation, was not what the public ultimately got to read. Initially unwelcome, then subject to the author's own selective memory, the final version of *Naked Among Wolves* had still to pass the tough GDR censors. The SED leadership and the politicians of memory working on the myth of Buchenwald were now by no means unaware of the symbolic capital to be earned from the novel. A suitably modulated novel speaking to the East German people would be a very welcome gift for the Ulbricht clique in its urgently needed efforts to consolidate its power. But

the plans the Party had for Buchenwald called for an absolutely unblemished version of the Buchenwald story. *Naked
Among Wolves* was passed through the censorship mill, sieved
and filtered, every ambivalence removed and rewritten as
a populist political tale. The version of the book that finally
went on sale was a narration exclusively about a cohesive
Communist fighting group built on solidarity, martyrdom and
self-emancipation.

A flawed book, a flawed memory and an author left to himself
and his recollections, who when asked in an interview who had
edited his book, replied in just two words: 'Walter Ulbricht'.
Despite or maybe because of this, *Naked Among Wolves* was
a spectacular success. The East German readers were grateful
to accept the book. It became an official reference work. It
turned the East Germans into a society of victims bound by
solidarity and into 'history's winners', pure and noble, without
any conflicting feelings of guilt or complicity.

The Buchenwald National Memorial opened in September
1958 with full ideological fanfare. It was a date that was des-
tined to establish the stronghold housing the collective identity
of the GDR. The evening before, GDR radio broadcast a play
based on the novel. In 1960 came the first documentary about
Buchenwald followed by a television adaptation. In 1963 the
DEFA film *Nackt unter Wölfen* was released in East German
cinemas and by the beginning of 1964 had been seen by one
million cinemagoers. In 1970 the novel was included in the
GDR high school syllabus and was read thereafter by all year
9 pupils.

The staccato Buchenwald refrain had become established
as an immutable state doctrine, a policy of memory that hyp-
notized millions of East Germans and made them loyal to the
GDR, not least because it dealt with and subsequently cemented
the deep underlying mental attitude of the post-fascist GDR:
withhold, explain away, reinterpret, trivialize, blank out,
avoid, forget. They were the mimicry strategies offered by the

authorities and accepted by the majority consciousness. The pressure was enormous. East Germany effectively established itself in this basic psycho-historical scene. It was so ineluctable that it constituted a form of self-preservation. It was the outer skin of its political consciousness.

REGROUPING. At peak viewing time in April 2015, to mark the seventieth anniversary of the liberation of Buchenwald, the national public television network ARD broadcast the new version of the film *Nackt unter Wölfen.* MDR,[3] which was responsible for the film, announced explicitly that it was not a remake of the DEFA film but a 'new interpreta-tion'. The producers were hoping for a 'new inter-German debate on anti-fascism'. The *Mitteldeutsche Zeitung,* the *Tagesspiegel* and the *SUPERillu* reported on the shooting of the film in Vojna[4] in the Czech Republic. The *Sächsische Zeitung* warned: 'There is a considerable risk that this new version from MDR will confuse the viewers' culture of memory or turn it on its head.' The film received strong and effusive reviews. 'A revision of the anti-fascist bible,' wrote *Die Zeit.* 'A recalibration of the original anti-fascist meter,' conjectured *Die Welt.*

The screenwriter Stefan Kolditz, born in East Germany, said in an interview that the film could help to unite the still disparate collective memory in the East and West. The key scene in the film shows the small Jewish boy. His hand is touching the head of the dying Communist who rescued him. The film concludes by conflating the suffering of the Jews and the Communists. A blatant historical distortion. Historical research at the time of the production would have served to destroy the Buchenwald myth. But it was not to be.

[3] Mitteldeutscher Rundfunk – the regional television network of the states of eastern Germany.
[4] A former Communist Gulag where political opponents were imprisoned and murdered.

In many of the scenes in the film, the film makers follow the original version of the novel published in 2014 and reconstruct in Bruno Apitz's earlier transitory memories: a much more ambiguous camp life, the absence of heroic self-liberation, and a red resistance network that was not all-knowing but rather marked by anxiety and despotism. But this 'new interpretation' still ran up against the brick wall erected by the former Buchenwald inmates in 1945. A highly idiosyncratic generational narrative? In the midst of this new attention to the revised version of his book, the film, documentary and biography, Bruno Apitz was restyled with astonishing verve by his biographer Lars Förster as an 'opponent of three German states'.

CHILDHOOD ORGAN

For Robby there is only one city, only one river, only these wild embankments, the Loschwitz Bridge, the steamships, only one tram line, the 11, only the Yenidze, the tobacconist where grandmother rolled cigarettes, only his sherbet powder under the pillow, only the crumbling fat putti in front of the house. He doesn't want ever to leave Dresden. To buy the last pieces of cake for five pfennigs from George the baker in the Weisser Hirsch district, to look out for lizards at the Obelisk, to linger in the streets with me and immerse himself in the endless story of light: the old spa building, the ballroom, the stucco, the revolving doors, towers, mirrors, terraces. The former lustre has been pasted over in blue and green. And we have nothing better to do than to watch the light as it dissipates.

And then to carry on roaming. The fisherwoman on the Sonnenleite. Villa San Remo with its luminous green pointed roof. The Erholung beer tavern, where we stand at the counter on Sundays with the pewter jug and order three litres of draught beer for father. The toothless woman from Materniweg with her horses and cows, the troughs and foul stench. The childhood organ known only to us two. Where we act as if we were free. A huge world that needs no explanation. When we roam the streets we don't talk. And now, round the corner and we're home.

A growing void

DENSITY. Ivy and moss in the back courtyard, the large wooden shed where, to judge by the smell, mildew is the sole inhabitant. The grand piano in the living room, the Blüthner piano in the children's room. The Loschwitz Bridge down in the valley, Rondo Melange and Hansa biscuits, the clarinet, the bassoon, the trumpet, the flutes, the triangle, the two accordions. A world of beauty and sound. In my brother's work diary, which he kept while studying art, he wrote in 1997: 'We always used to play in this courtyard, and this is the site of my memories. There are mountains of pictures in my albums and boxes: my sister building a snowman, me on a tricycle, both of us in a tepee, in the old plastic bathtub or in the sandpit. Mother in the strawberry beds, the old garden swing, the tall oak with the rabbit hutch at its foot. Perhaps the old photos could be set alongside the new ones. The latticed windows that used to be there and now emphasize the inaccessibility of the places of my childhood. I'm sad. The oak tree has been cut down.'

In his diary there are also quotes from Roland Barthes: 'As if the horror of Death were not precisely its platitude! The horror is this: nothing to say about the death of one whom I love most, nothing to say about her photograph, which I contemplate without ever being able to get to the heart of it, to transform it.' That which can't be transformed, that which is unique. I browse in Robby's boxes of photos, just as I used to roam with him through the Weisser Hirsch. There is an endless amount of material, masses of negatives, much more than can ever be developed. What did he plan to do with it? Keep a record of his entire life?

My brother and his photos, his photo cycles, series, rows. His exhibitions in Dresden. His notes that looked for the disruptions, empty spaces, degrees of compactness. 'The formal intensity determines the degree of compactness of the sentence,' he wrote in his diary. A strange sentence. As if something is trying to get out but then has to disappear again immediately. I rummage further. In one box there are just photos of dolls. Shiny pink arms, fleshy thighs, uniformly round heads. Those eyes! Strangely constructed and blurred at the same time. Creepy, I find. But then I don't like dolls. At the bottom of the box are two sheets of paper. Robby writes: 'It is the magic of the light on the doll, but also its silent testimony to my childhood. The blurring is the reflection of the confusion arising in me.'

The light, which always has to do with bodies. The memory that is somehow unyielding. The photos that don't invent reality but have to connect with it. But above all the thing with the blurring, the confusion, and Robby with his phantom dolls. What was he looking for with them? 'The reading of photos, the narration of the context takes into account the rules of remembering, see parents.' See parents? Is there a parent box? Where is it? My goodness, there are three of them.

NEW BEGINNINGS. In the first one, father is sitting on a sprawling stone balustrade. 'Summer 1954,' it says on the photo. Behind him the huge portraits of Stalin, Ulbricht, Pieck. A twenty-year-old and Albrechtsberg Palace on the banks of the Elbe in Dresden, which three years earlier was founded as the first Soviet-style pioneers palace, named 'Walter Ulbricht'. The paved driveway, the fountain, the young ensemble director waiting for his choir in front of the sonorous surging water. The bus was parked waiting, ready to take them from Dresden to Weimar. The road continued up from there through the forest to the Ettersberg. They would stay there for three days to help erect the Buchenwald monument. Removing rubble, digging up the earth. That's when it all started, said my father one time. He really said it.

Mother and father, Brigitte Grunert and Lothar Geipel, two war children from Saxony, born in 1935 and 1934, who met in this Dresden pioneers palace. She was training to be a typesetter, he was studying music and longed to become a pianist. They married in 1953. The twenty-year-old with his choir, his young love, his studies and the absent father, said to be missing. When I went as a child to my other grandmother, it was to a woman waiting with dogged patience. On the sideboard was a framed photo of a man in a grey-green uniform. Sometimes he needed to be talked to. More precisely, grandmother with her snow-white hair needed to talk, and I was meant to be this man, whom I would never meet. I was meant to ask some questions about her life: how the aunts were, what was going on in Vogtland or Klingenthal, and whether she still had the Ford they had bought in 1935 for their marriage. At the end I always had to ask if she was all right and whether I, in other words he, should come home. When I went to boarding school at the age of fourteen, Robby took over this role.

In 2017, the German Office for Notification of Relatives of Members of the German Wehrmacht Killed in Action wrote about my second forefather, my father's father, a piano maker from the Vogtland region: 'In reply to your inquiry about the whereabouts of your grandfather Walter Geipel, born 4 March 1906 in Steindöbra, I hereby inform you he was a member of the 2nd Battery of the SS Police Mountain Artillery in the Belgrade area and has been missing since 14 October 1944.

Nothing further is known here about his whereabouts.' Two
short sentences with more information than grandmother and
father would ever have divulged about the missing person.

HARDWARE. Ulbricht proclaimed socialism in East Berlin
in 1952. A year later Stalin died in Moscow. Prior to that,
the young republic had experienced one purge after another.
Heads rolled right, left and centre. First in the party itself,
before the paranoia spread to every corner of the land. Trials,
expulsions, arrests, murders, deportations, dismissals, spe-
cious accusations. Between mid-1952 and mid-1953 alone,
some 500,000 East Germans fled to the West. The country
appeared to consist solely of enemies of the people, who were
to be dispatched with all due haste. The population was silent
about the Nazi period, and the returnees from Moscow were
silent about the Soviet terror. A furtive pact that exonerated
both sides and provided a basis for the purges. It was the hardware for the GDR system of fear and the condition for its
continuance. In the early GDR the slightest hint of criticism,
contradiction, difference, independent ideas or free thinking
had to be expunged. There was only one system of thought
and only two categories: friend or foe, good or evil, right or
wrong, victory or defeat. If you didn't belong to one world,
you automatically belonged to the other. Dictators – Stalin,
Mao, Ulbricht – all rely on their machinery for making people
disappear. Show trials were prepared in the GDR for the
editors-in-chief of all major newspapers and radio stations –
just as in 1937. It was only with Stalin's death and the popular
uprising of 17 June 1953, in which one and a half million East
Germans in 700 towns and cities participated, that the madness could be stopped.

And the essence of those years? So many studies, so many
thick books, so many sources. Destinies, scenes from overcrowded camps, prisons, shootings in Moscow, deportations
to the Gulag. But the images of the post-war period in East

Germany shown in the media today are still mostly ones of cheering. As if there was a double standard with regard to sources. As if the enthusiasm for Hitler could be seen immediately for what it was but the Ulbricht celebration was still accepted as the story of a better new beginning. As if an ideological cloud still hung over the beginning in the East.

DISMAY. The twenty-year-old choirmaster. He was eleven years old when the war ended, fifteen when the new state was founded. A war child who became part of the classic new generation, the ones the sociologists Annegret Schüle, Thomas Ahbe and Rainer Griesthe described as 'most closely connected with the ups and downs of the GDR's development, who built their careers in and with the GDR'. But what does that mean?

A generation socialized through Hitler, growing up in the ruins, with only dead, missing or disoriented parents, untrustworthy teachers, the collapse of all authorities, and a fear-ridden future. Battered but still having to negotiate the post-war vacuum. From 1948 to 1952, Lothar Geipel trained at the Klingenthaler Harmonienwerke, from 1952 he was pioneer leader on the Auerbach Free German Youth (FDJ) district committee, from 1951 he was FDJ head and ensemble director in the Dresden pioneers palace, and from 1954, at the age of twenty, he became a member of the SED.

The young activists, or 'white years'[1] – in their blue shirts, moving to new places, onto major construction sites, into party training centres and pioneers palaces, becoming new teachers and in a few cases building careers later on as chairmen of the State Council, winners of the Peace Race[2] or GDR cosmonauts. A generation marked by National Socialism, cheering and Hitler Youth, who feverishly supported 'Führer, Volk

[1] 'Weisse Jahrgänge' – age group not required to perform compulsory military service.
[2] Established after the war as the largest amateur cycling race in Eastern Europe.

and Vaterland' and dreamed of adventure, new beginnings and community. It was precisely this that the better Germany offered to this generation. The cheering was unbounded, as if the young Nazis were spurring each other on. In 1948 some 3,000 FDJ officials transferred to the SED organization.

Within this organization, however, were the old stagers, the political despots who had survived all of the struggles, during the Weimar period, under the Nazis and in exile. They promised the young generation that they could advance, but only if they followed the party diktat, proved themselves loyal and forgetting, and joined in spinning the propaganda wheel. In the early 1950s, most of the unrepentant old Communists had been purged from the 'new style party' and replaced by old and young Nazis. 'Instead of fascism as German socialism, there is now scientific Marxism,' the inquisitor and politburo member Hermann Matern assured the new arrivals. 'It will achieve what the other was unable to do.'

The post-fascist GDR of the 1950s was a synthesis between an encapsulated Hitler and the new dictatorship, as the solid foundation for what was to come, as its affective space, which is succeeding in forcing its way so vocally into today's political arena. Peter Sloterdijk described cultures as 'atmospheric systems' for which the 'creation of a microsphere' is particularly crucial. The microsphere of East Germany. It comes from that time of forming, formatting, honing and manic angst. A time of shock that outwardly celebrated the future while hollowing out what was inside, underneath and behind so thoroughly that we have forgotten it.

Studie IV, a film by Peter Weiss made in 1954: A man searches in a box for papers. They promise to explain his situation and feelings. He leaves them unread. Instead, we see his hands tearing up the sheets. He goes to the window, opens it, looks down and throws the pieces into the courtyard. The camera follows the shreds as they blow away until they are merely white dots. *Studie IV* has the title 'liberation'. But how to achieve liberation? The space for forgetting of the 1950s, the continuing confusion and the East German Pavlov cult. When the GDR was founded, Freudian psychoanalysis was thrown overboard, or more precisely banned, as a 'barbaric anti-humanistic ideology'. But a replacement was desperately needed. How can the new world succeed if those who are making it cannot overcome their guilt? How to provide without psychological underpinning for the millions of desolate souls marked by war so that they could devote all of their energy to rewriting their history? When the situation in East Germany became unbearable, it was deliberately anaesthetized. In the early phase of the GDR this was done with comatose sleep, from the 1960s with chemicals, and at the end of the GDR with ionizing radiation.

SUBLOOPS. In 1950, Stalin made the conditioning model of the Russian physiologist Ivan Pavlov the absolute basis for Marxist psychology. 'Sleep is extended inhibition,' wrote Pavlov. His concept aimed directly at the brain, at the 'controlling and organizing role of the cerebral cortex', or more precisely at the 'dictatorship of the cortex'. Sleeping chambers were set up in great style in East Germany and test subjects put to sleep. A striking image: the subjects did not lie on the couch of memory but crowded into the sleeping chambers of forgetting. Laboratories that soon became a cult. To recover finally from the stress of the new state, to sleep away the trauma, and, at least in the subloops of the mind, to obtain relief from suffering and responsibility. Healing through sleep.

There are all kinds of photos of the new men and women leaving their sleep laboratories and the weeks of amnesia. Young people waking up and stretching in the morning after a deep sleep, jumping out of bed, doing their early morning exercises, drinking a glass of milk with evident enjoyment and then stepping out in top form to face the day – very hearty, very energetic, very dutiful. Rise and shine! That's how Communism goes, every day afresh. Even if total anaesthesia such as this inevitably had its limits and Pavlov disappeared extensively from the public view in 1957, the dozing 1950s helped East Germany to get through an extremely delicate period. How else to be fully conscious and still put up with the kill-or-cure structural changes, the terror and the publicly visible insanity of the regime but also with the personal self-delusion? 'Inhibition is local sleep,' said Pavlov. But what parts of the body had to be anaesthetized to get through the years after the war? For what inner refuges was uninhibited sleep ordered so that some pressure could finally escape from the cooker to enable the population to survive the hardship and somehow continue?

UNSTRUCK STRINGS. What happened next? I can visualize my parents in their first apartment in the Weisser Hirsch district. My father pulling open the balcony door, my mother inspecting the cooker and the large coal stoves, both of my parents standing on the terrace looking at each other and nodding. This is what's called seed capital, this type of generosity, the view into the valley, Villa San Remo with its green shimmering pointed roof directly opposite, and the neighbours right and left – painters, singers, architects, doctors, composers. This could work, don't you think?

Time passes, the images disappear. I try to imagine the apartment when it was still empty, when my parents scaled the heights, ran through the cool air, built into the forest, between salamanders, polecats and alkaline springs. Where everything came from the ground ('Grund') and was inevitably in every name: Grundstrasse, Grundleite, Grundweg. I try to consider what was actually the 'ground' in this apartment. And I have to say something again about the sound, the many instruments, the mountains of musical scores, father's chorists, who regularly sat around the grand piano. I have to explain it all, I want finally to understand it. And the aliquot strings of the Blüthner piano, which I later practised on. Aliquot strings, what a name! How can anyone remember that? Three strings, explained father opening the lid, have to be struck to make a sound. The fourth string simply vibrates with them, it's just there. The aliquot system in Saxon pianos – one unstruck string per note. That's what gives it the dusky sound, the resonance, some say the secret.

This aliquot sound in the air, which opened up the view of the land: the extensive sight of the shattered but still recognizable silhouette of Dresden, the slow-flowing Elbe threading its way through the valley beneath. A bit further on, in the city centre, grandfather was sitting in his armchair. He was almost completely unresponsive. It was as if the corner of the living room where he had installed himself for years had swallowed him up. Grandmother, by contrast, was as if electrified. Her Konsum store on Fetscherplatz was flourishing. She managed it as she had organized the care of the wounded in the hospital in Riga. A woman who knew how to give orders, who was always on duty, for whom what she called law and order had priority over everything. In 1956 she celebrated her fiftieth birthday.

Perhaps she looked back briefly and saw the girl who waved at the Saxon king's coach. Then the young woman who worked herself to the bone during the Weimar period trying to find some solid ground under her feet. And finally the woman with the Gold Cross of Honour who gave Hitler any number of children, of whom six were now trying somehow to find their way under Ulbricht. At the end of the war she wrote the famous letter to Hitler's chief ideologist Alfred Rosenberg. Just two years later, the addressee was hanged as one of the major war criminals in Nuremberg. What did she think at that moment? What did the Nazi women think, do and say ten years later under the new dictatorship? Was the system a rupture for them? Grandmother had become manager of a Konsum shop. A Konsum in the GDR was a public place, a sort of stage. Many lives came together there. Food, everyday existence, need, words. At least Hitler had true charisma, said grandmother to the very end.

That's not what comes to mind initially in connection with the East German experiment. But it was said, and sounds to me today like a witness of the past. Where could the habit of belief, the urge to idolize, the massive denial of reality disappear to so quickly after the war? No word from grandmother about the time in Riga. Her decision had long been made: she wanted to ensure that her family survived. In fact, it was not really a conscious decision, because grandmother would just have called it her life. Something that was there. What else could she have done? For her there were no systems, no rupture and also no political responsibility. Society was like nature, cyclical but ultimately immutable. Grandmother's philosophy of life was work. And there was always work. She also had a certain soft spot. And that was for Hitler.

I can see grandmother standing quite upright in the door of her Konsum shop. I see her waving. A gaunt and purposeful woman who never allowed herself to be sick, ate little and drank no alcohol. Who made you wash in cold water in the morning, who pointed out mistakes all the time and did not tolerate even white lies. Who knew what she wanted and had found herself. She led. She set the tone wherever she was. We went with her to her office. We rolled the coins in hard brown packing paper, examined purchasing lists, checked the Konsum brands. Was there enough of everything? There was lots to do until everything was completely right. Until then there was no question of going home, that was for sure.

WOMEN'S POLITICS. Privacy, history, crime and the politics of women. How far is it from grandmother with the Gold Cross of Honour to the myth of the fully emancipated East German woman? There are, of course, lots of smiling and waving women in the celebratory photos of the 1950s. A time of new formats, women's brigades, women workers with throaty voices, who joined the hundreds of young activists on major construction sites, in the untamed landscapes of East Germany, in the veritable deserts, who asked about the question of power in a completely different way. How to become liberated? Another revolution? Young women driving tractors, trams, excavators – all new professions and women, forcefully storming the streets of victory. Did they assume that nothing better was planned for them than for their success stories to shine amid the dark ranks of male politicians? 'Behind the cardboard façade a growing nothingness,' wrote the poet Inge Müller in 1957.

The new women, who pushed forward and in the same breath were incorporated in the accelerated memory-concretizing phase of the 1950s. Who came from flag-waving under Hitler, from devotion and self-sacrifice, and now sang Ulbricht's praises. Who had cheered at the mass demonstrations, the fluttering banners and swearing in of recruits during the Nazi period and now vigorously cheered the new Communist effort. They must inevitably have been in the majority and strong advocates of the young GDR. Social change? On the one hand there were the women's committees formed already in November 1945 by order of the Soviet military administration, and on the other hand the media power of the Deutscher Frauenverlag founded shortly after the end of the war. Together they were meant to concentrate and organize the female energy. Of the 28,000 rubble clearers in Berlin, 22,000 were women. The Ulbricht clan needed women as working, in other words economically independent, 'builders of socialism' and contrasted them demonstratively with the back-to-the-kitchen policy imposed on women in the West, where the reactionaries and their reactionary women were. Where no one had revolution in mind.

The first constitution of the GDR in October 1949 called for equality of men and women before the law, equal right to work, equal pay for equal work and special protection for women, marriage and family. So much for ideology. In the land of work, however, the tight triad of work, children and family – the principle of extreme multitasking – prevailed, not least to make women permanent spectators of power. A gender policy that was perfect for coordinating the synchronization of the GDR state and its inhabitants.

ILLUMINATED GONDOLAS

A long stairway down, a long stairway up, and Robby and I are at the top, at the entrance to the Dresden funicular railway. The high hallway, the wooden benches, the large suspended clock, the people who come from below, from Körnerplatz, and just want to go home. Robby proudly presents the mark coin in his hand. It's enough for five rides up and down. And where is yours? We get in and hold on tight. Our children's minds are clearly thinking of the disaster that awaits us. It's our game: something is bound to go wrong. Or not? We give each other a wink. The cabin jerks, starts moving, squeals and leaves the top station. We enter the top tunnel. Something's bound to go wrong, whispers my brother in the darkness. Sparkling dark green water drips from the stones. We come out of the tunnel into the daylight.

The yellow gondola makes its way over the long hump of the Elbe slope. Below us the city, floating as if in a trance. The overhead wires crackle. To the left and right are old quince trees, exuding the aroma of childhood. Look, shouts Robby, jumping up and pointing to the second gondola still loitering in the valley below. The cable bites and lurches. Here come the points. The two cabins like swaying boats, like travelling com-panions, like two people who are not quite sure of themselves but are nevertheless heading blindly for one another. They make an effort, they approach one another, they will inevitably meet up at the halfway point.

My brother chews his lower lip, breathing in time with the swaying and clattering of the gondolas. Here it comes, he says, here it comes, and screws his eyes closed. We hold our breath. The cabin rattles, groans, teeters over the edge of the valley. We're going to fall. It's bound to happen. The entire slope is creaking. Suddenly the other gondola is right next to us. Robby fiddles with his t-shirt, completely silent, observing the two yellow gondolas as they pass within a hair's breadth of one another. The passengers wave as if slipping over the edge were the most normal thing in the world. There's nothing to hold on to. A man in the other gondola jumps up and yells at us: Ship ahoy!

A second later and we're alone again. The journey immediately takes on a different form. We've passed the hump and are heading directly downwards. It feels as if we have been abandoned. Robby looks behind him. The other gondola is creeping up the slope like a valiant insect. It's because of us that it can do that, he proclaims proudly and gives me a nudge: we got away with it again.

Versions of a father

DIVISIONS. My brother's death was the most improbable thing. It came completely unexpectedly. That's the least I can say. As long as I existed, there was Robby as well. Simple as that. Because he existed, childhood had stars, islands, gondolas. With him there was freedom, gentleness, moving. When I think of him, he is snuggling up to me, dozing, dreaming, rabbiting on a bit. I liked that and needed it. We were together, as simple as that. In our own space. Not in my wildest dreams did I imagine my brother dying. I didn't know it was possible. In truth I had never given it any thought. That sounds absurd: as if life were a question of years.

And it bothers me. How could such a certainty have existed without me having taken the trouble even once to name it seriously? Was I not bothered by it? Was I unable to do it? Only today, when every day reminds me that Robby has gone, is it clear that there was something wrong with this construct. It was not a question of closeness. That was never in doubt. It had to do with something behind it or behind what might be called familiar territory. Something that was so fundamental that it was shapeless, timeless, on its own and unaffected by anything. What was it? How could Robby's death have been such a shock for me, although I hadn't seen him for five years? He was my brother, that's true, but was that all?

It's not easy to write about the fabric between remembering and forgetting. Where am I? How to get through this tangled undergrowth? Where does it end? Perhaps we don't remember because we are unable to solve the problem with the images. There are too many. Perhaps remembering is not remembering at all because what we remember is in any case there all the time. And there must be other good reasons why we question everything that calls itself memory. At all events, my brother's death was like a beacon. Suddenly everything was there again. Like a flash of memory. Images, words, odours – everything came ceaselessly rushing at me. What was there between Robby and me? Basically it could only have been one thing: in our childhood we offered each other a place to hide. Anything we didn't understand, anything we had to keep, we placed it with the other. There it was protected and could survive. Robby's death suddenly changed the situation. Something of myself remained in him and had to be extracted, if it wasn't to be buried with him. Families are high-calibre affairs and councils of loyalty. So what was going on with us two?

Robby's parent boxes. In the first one are the beginnings, in the second what we might call roots. Some of the contents ran in parallel. I was born in July 1960, and the cut-off came in August 1961. The Wall was built and the country encapsulated. Everything was tightly sealed. For some it was a new declaration of war, others hoped it would be a turning point and the moment to start building 'proper socialism'. The historian Gerd Koenen later called the division of the country 'the principal means for coming to terms with the past'. If the country hadn't been torn apart, the psychological legacy of National Socialism could not have been dealt with. Sixteen years after the end of the war, the country was split in two, and those things that could not be integrated in one side were transferred to the other. Sixteen years of cleaning up, keeping silent and rewriting. Instead of a shared history, there was now a divided land. But the questions and doubts remained. The victims were silent, but would they remain so? The need to keep living had covered over the memories, but wouldn't they have to break out sometime? When? In twenty, thirty or even fifty years? And what would happen to the country when it was sometime allowed to have its full memory back again?

SET IN STONE. The Wall as a political litmus test. Those years of division – not only outward but also inward – must have been strange and often bitter. Those who in the 1950s had quarrelled fiercely about the situation in the country in beer cellars, canteens, private homes, gardens or dachas often no longer met. The selection was mostly tacit. Those who said yes to the state knew about those who had turned their backs on it, and vice versa. The country was small, the scenes manageable. To refuse meant not to get on in the GDR. It meant not to calmly accept the separation of families and of a country. It meant loss of life, obstructed careers, isolation. The split was inexorable. Quite a few fell through the crack.

The 11th Plenary Session of the SED Central Committee just before Christmas 1965 became famous, and not in a good way. Instead of more openness, it was back to restriction and pressure through a brutal proxy cultural battle. Among the artists there were now only counter-revolutionaries, revisionists, nihilists and decadents. The prohibitions rained down. Twelve DEFA films – an entire year's production – disappeared into the poison cabinet. Plays, novels and bands were also banned. The older generation, voices such as Anna Seghers or Kurt Barthels, wearily submitted to this intellectual obeisance as a kind of déjà-vu, the latest round in the eternal scenario of ruling party vetoes. For the younger ones, such as Werner Bräunig or Christa Wolf, the cultural butchery was a heavy blow. Dismayed and disillusioned, they distanced themselves seriously for the first time from their GDR identity project.

The same was true of most of the East German war children's generation, who must have realized that through this cultural scorched earth policy the regime was demonstrating that it was not capable of serious corrective measures and that by building the Wall something had once again quite literally been set in stone. They reacted to this inflexibility by withdrawing.

Is all this necessary? Is there a need for this political perspective to somehow get closer to Robby? Yes, absolutely. It is the reflection of the internal denial. As if history and personal feelings pull each other like the two gondolas on the slopes of the Elbe that are trying to get better acquainted. They are conditional on one another, mutually dependent. These up and down journeys are needed as well because the family keeps private matters and history so strictly separate. My brother was born in 1967. In 1968, the Prague Spring and the stifled revolution, which for many people brought paralysis, disillusionment and a farewell to the utopian illusion. This spring marked the end of the GDR for them. For the builders, the young Nazis, the terrible fear returned that the historically superlative GDR could fail after all. This was the parent generation, who had allowed themselves to be corrupted, who had built careers, who were deeply implicated in the system. And now, how to continue? Or how to get out? Something had to happen. Because the parvenus realized that Prague 1968 was not just a few uncomfortable images, it was the watershed, the breach, the harbinger of the end of Ulbricht. His era was over. What did that mean? The country had arrived at the innermost chamber of a closed society.

SURVEYING. Father and mother. When the Wall was built they were still young, just over thirty. He was now working as a music teacher and from 1967 was principal of a newly built polytechnic college on the Elbe. I sometimes visited him there and was met by a man with his jacket undone, dynamic, with a loud voice, his world completely and unconditionally marked out. Four years later he became deputy head of the district school board. On 1 May I would sit on his shoulders. Blond with a military haircut. He stood on the large platform in front of the town hall. Red paper pennants everywhere, red plastic carnations in the lapels, and father with a microphone in his hand: 'Chemists, work hard to use up all by-products! Railwaymen, take good care of your rolling stock!' And in between, he cheered: 'Hurrah, hurrah, hurrah!' The street shook and echoed.

Time goes backwards and stops with me. There is a level from which we observe history. It offers distance and safety. Better not to get too involved. But I stayed seated on father's shoulders, as he droned endlessly into the microphone: 'And in marching formation comes block' something or other. His shoulders swayed and wobbled, I slid from one side to the other, my hands held tightly to his head as if it were a buoy in the sea. Soon I was aching all over. I needed to pee.

The thing with Robby's boxes of photos and my notes, which now also seem to me like two gondolas. I wonder whether Robby had any kind of order in his boxes. In his last summer he digitized everything. Did he put the photos back where he found them? Were they arranged chronologically? Or were they sorted according to how important they were for him at the end? I don't know. The second parent box contains almost only colour photos: mother, Robby and me in a sand hollow on the Baltic, Robby and me on the steps in the garden with oval soap bubbles, father giving a talk at the Urania, my brother and I as flower children at various weddings. We both look very serious, me still with the stupid woollen stockings bulging loosely at the knee.

The wedding groups: women with short hair and flowing petticoat dresses, men in dark suits with white or black bow ties, the children anaemic and evidently lacking sleep, at any rate with dark shadows under their eyes. Large private functions in Dresden in the early 1970s. With a note from Robby:

'When presenting the photos at an exhibition, I would place the pictures close together without mountings so that they touch each other. This would perhaps best reflect the diversity of relationships. I'm still not sure how I should make the connection on the wall with the series underneath, maybe in groups next to and underneath one another or in rows underneath and next to each other.'

Cycles, series, groups. Robby writes that for him photos are principally a possibility for 'surveying' the world around him. My gaze stops at one photo. It shows father's study. I have often thought about him and his music. That he always had something in his life that was alive and fulfilled him. The sounds, the instruments, the scores, the choirs. It was his main interest, but did he really like it? I can see myself sitting at the Blüthner piano with a mark coin on the back of either hand. He is behind me, asking me the notes, correcting my posture from top to bottom, hands held out so that the coins don't fall. I can see myself in the knowledge that it can't possibly end well.

The photo of the interior. With timpani, bassoon, grand piano, the two accordions, the music stands. All a little bit posed. As if it was the intermission. And the couch, the bookshelf, the television set. In the background, barely visible, grandfather's velvet armchair. The back of the photo is marked '1973'. I remember mother coming to me in the bathroom, closing the door behind her and announcing that grandfather had died that day. He was running for the bus and his heart tore apart. He fell down and was dead on the spot. No one could have done anything for him. His armchair is in the background in the photo. It looks almost like a spectre. As absent as grandfather had been. The day when mother told me in the bathroom about his death was 21 May 1972, father's birthday. I remember exactly.

TECTONIC SHIFTS. Looking back, it's difficult to determine whether the changes were already there at this time but were keeping a low profile so as to become even more visible later. Or whether they were still unknown to themselves and came about blindly without warning. I'm talking about father and his time as a Stasi agent. This is what happened. Grandfather's armchair ended up in father's study, probably in summer 1972. The country had a new head, Erich Honecker. He spoke of realignment and a 'socialist German nation state'. It was during this time that the GDR was also recognized diplomatically throughout the world. That is what was said at the time. Outward calm, but a fragile internal situation. The effects of Prague 1968 were still being felt. Above all, this brought Stasi boss Erich Mielke onto the scene with his plans for endowing this chronically unstable country with a modern secret service. He held a speech in secret in July 1972 in which he announced the end of the ruthless suppression and purges of the early GDR years and called for more subtle, discreet and clandestine repression. It was more than ever necessary to separate the wheat from the chaff, he said, and pointed to the new strategies he had devised. He named two of these strategies: *Zersetzung* or decomposition,[1] and isolation. To achieve these aims, he claimed, he needed a large number of new recruits. A tectonic shift within the country so as to make the brutality more targeted and ensure that the system would not have to be changed in any way.

Among the 'new recruits' was my father. In March 1972 he became head of the Dresden pioneers palace. Just a month later, he had a meeting in his office with two Stasi men. They noted in their report that 'Geipel is on the move for days on end and is not accountable to anyone. To that extent he can carry out tasks at any time and is thus of operative interest for us.' It's not easy to write this, but it belongs here: how in December 1973 – the official GDR Pioneers Day – he signed

---

[1] Systematic degrading, discrediting and undermining the self-confidence, prestige or reputation of victims.

up to work for Department IV of the Stasi. How he expounded at great length in his declaration of commitment on what good would come from his new job. How, from then on, he met Stasi people in car parks on Dresden Heath, in Café Toscana, in the HO-Gaststätte 'Szeged', in the Rosengarten, at the newspaper stand on Zwinglistrasse, in countless conspiratorial apartments – Stübel, Schäfer, Iris – and carried out all the missions they had thought up for him. 'Geipel appears to have no inhibitions. He knows what he wants and is able to see it through,' acknowledged his handler.

KNOCKOUTS. This sounds dangerous, and it was at that. Who are you if you have no inhibitions? Father's thick Stasi file contains all kinds of complex missions and training. I read that he quickly 'built up confidence in the organ' and felt 'closely attached to the organ'. The organ – for organisation. I think of the liver and kidneys, of something inside me that does its job unnoticed, that is vulnerable and at risk. I knew of no organ that would make someone dangerous. But father's organ was just that. It summoned him many times to Berlin. There were meetings at the flower stand in the forecourt of the Ostbahnhof. From there he and the organ travelled to a military camp. Father had combat training. There were dummies, climbing walls, tracking, karate for the knockout blow and additional training with a camera. What was it all about? Father was forty years old. I try to imagine how, somewhere outside Berlin, he gasped his way through the obstacle course, grilled his dummies and attempted at night to drill into himself his future pseudo-biographies. I can't manage it.

But he seems to have managed, because from December 1973 he travelled regularly to the 'operative territory' in the West. He was now an instructor with different names, depending on the mission – Gerhard Kirchner, Gerhard André, Norbert Simon or Gerd Krüger. According to his passport, Gerhard Kirchner was a year younger than father, a widower, born in Chemnitz

and a music teacher living in Stübelallee in Dresden. Norbert
Simon was six months younger, born in Nuremberg, a pianist
and living in Wiesbaden. Eight different names, eight different
passports, eight different identities. How many people is there
room for in one person? I don't know if I want to think about
it. In father's file there are also mountains of secret service
stories, observations and counter-observations, meeting places
and meeting systems, identifying marks, escape routes, pass-
words, contingency plans, all-clear signals, warning signals. As
if father were moving in a labyrinth that became narrower,
denser and more confusing with every mission. Story 1: 'I would
like to apply to the Städtische Bühnen in Frankfurt/Main as a
pianist.' – Contingency plan 3: 'Two hours later or the next day
at the same time.' – Identifying mark 6: 'Sunglasses with light
metal rim and one arm protruding from the top left suit jacket
pocket (3 cm).' – Warning signal 8: 'At the postcard stand,
turning or looking around, holding a postcard.'

What is a man without inhibitions? I assume that you have
to put in some effort and that it is by no means easy to become
one. That it's hard work and takes time. In fact I don't really
know. But father was without inhibitions from the outset. That,
at least, is the assessment of his handler. This was welcomed by
the secret service. It could exploit it because father could be
manipulated at will as a result. A man without inhibitions who
for fifteen years crossed over the border between two enemy
systems, who carried out a variety of missions under eight
different names in all kinds of places in the 'operative territory': as Gerhard in Marburg he contacted Heinz Paulsen, a
Stasi agent in the West; as Norbert in Cologne he spied on the
Emonts company; as Gerd in Porz he identified someone; as
Hans he reconnoitred apartment buildings in West Berlin and
a garage in Freiburg. As someone or other he trudged through
deep snowdrifts, crawled through tunnels, jumped over walls,
took any number of photos and tracked refugees from the
East who had managed somehow to escape. He drew sketches

of their houses, took photos of their children on the way to school, investigated their new places of work. Father never knew exactly what his missions were about. 'The IM [unofficial collaborator] was given no information about the purpose and duration of the journey.' This means that he had no idea of the power structure he was involved in. But he delivered the goods perfectly. Why? Did he not realize that there was a world he knew nothing about? Did he have so few scruples that he didn't care?

Father's detailed handwritten reports, all of which are on file, are unending, precise and without a single mistake. No trace of inhibition. He appears highly concentrated. So as not to be distracted or lose control? The 'organ' noted: 'Gerhard always appeared calm and collected before his missions. He gave not the slightest indication of excitement or nerves.' How often have I tried to imagine this. Was he afraid? Did it ever get critical? Which part of father was when, where and how? What was he doing in the Waldecker Hof in Marburg three days before Christmas 1974? What was he thinking as he sat in the Berlin Philharmonic? Was he just listening to the music? Did he understand the life he was leading? He was sometimes in the West for three or four weeks at a time. When we asked after him, mother said that he had been sent on a course. Where were we in his thoughts all this time? Where did he put his life of terror when he came back home?

EAGLE 1 OVER

I close my eyes and see hordes of woodlice and the chipboard they are lounging on and the corner of the garden with the least light. 'Shoo! Get away!' shouts my brother, waving in their direction. 'Get out of here.' We move the board to the side so that the light can reveal our two spaceships. How long we spent making them! All the things we dragged in for them! Tons of autumn grass from the meadow as insulation, branches lying around the garden for the cockpit, empty metal boxes for genuine radio messages. Jars, bags, cans for the treasures we needed to take with us into space: salamander skins, fish scales, snail shells, hair ties, paper clips, liquorice, sherbet powder.

Let's go, says Robby happily and jumps into his seat in the cockpit. I sit next to him in the capsule. My brother is responsible for the launch, I give instructions: brake off, throttle open. – Do you feel the pressure in your bones? he asks. – Yes, in the shoulders, chest, now the knees. – Good, he says, pulling the joystick. Me: Are we ready? Him: We'll soon reach the lowest point, the greatest pressure. We're lifting off. Look how the air moves apart. I'll count: ten metres, twenty, thirty, forty.

The instruments tick away and at some point the pressure goes away, the machine tips forward and we're up there, stretching our arms out, holding hands briefly. Only briefly, because we have to maintain altitude.

I hammer on my metal box and shout to the left: Eagle 1, what's wrong with you? Over! Robby answers: On course 370 for Saturn. Eagle 2, over! – I don't understand, I thought we were going to the lunar city. – No, we're headed for Saturn. Change of course. Pass the liquorice. – Do we have enough fuel? Eagle 1, over! No liquorice left. Only after Saturn.

Whatever way, Robby launches us into space. Everything is going well. No problems as far as the moon. After that it'll get difficult, but it doesn't matter. Not at all. We have each other.

SOUND MECHANICS

Father comes home from the antiques dealer on Bautzner Landstrasse. He has a broken music box. Every restored item becomes a piece of Meissen porcelain and ends up later in the baroque cabinet. Mother looks inside the cabinet and is amazed at all the items in there. For special days, she reckons.

Father places the package on the table. May I? asks Robby and unwraps it. A merry-go-round, my brother cries gleefully. Four horses and a red and white roof. Doesn't it work anymore? I ask. It's completely broken, explains father, and will have to be taken apart. There's a lot of work to be done. So off you go, he says, pointing to the bottom of the merry-go-round. That's where the cylinder is.

Fixing a music box is a tricky business. To be honest it's incredibly complicated. Father's hands are too big for what goes on in the clockwork mechanism. So he needs us. It's like a clock but it's not one, he explains, tapping his fingers nervously on the table. Loosen the four screws on the wooden housing and expose the comb. The pins mustn't touch the comb. The metal strips mustn't break. We solder, file, polish, tinker. We want to do it right. Every strip plays a different note and must be realigned. This is meticulous work. Father says nothing more, but his fingers speak. It's taking too long.

But he lets us work at it. Now it's the turn of the hairsprings. Remove the strands from the feather dampers. We're not even halfway through, we're only at the governor and Robby's already giving up. He's tired. What tune will it play when it's fixed? I ask. 'Du lieber Augustin',[2] says father. Robby strokes the colourful horses lying separately on the table. He lays his head on the table. I can't do any more, he says. He knows all the tunes on the cylinders. He babbles and keeps on repeating: 'Blouses gone, houses gone, how do we carry on?'

[2] 'Did You Ever See a Lassie?' is an English song with the same melody as 'Du lieber Augustin'.

Dolls are easy targets

ACUTE. At the end of May 1975 father sat in Café Kranzler in West Berlin, observed the Ku'damm, ate a slice of Sachertorte and drank tea. In early December 1976 he settled for lunch in Hotel Stephanie in Poststrasse, Freiburg, and ordered a schnitzel that was too big for him. In February 1979 he emptied the minibar in the Überseehotel in Bremen and then needed something to eat. He ordered Nuremberg sausages with potato salad. That's what it says in his file. Eating was important for father. He took it seriously. The same with his clothing. In the fifteen years of his service for the terror regime, the organ insisted that he dress for his missions in the 'normal style of the West'. The list of 'objects for personal needs as required' included fur hats, slippers, stockings, glasses, silk scarves. From 1975 father listed 'medicine for acute treatment', which cost around DM500 for every mission.

Father appreciated good food, beautiful objects and hard work, he needed music, he liked orgies and blowouts, but above all he was out to destroy other people. That was his passion. 'To take something seriously means to be concrete . . . because it is real. It can't be altered, it's tangible, it is something you have to get through,' says Ingmar Bergman. Robby and I had to put up with it. I don't mean getting a slap, being grounded or any of the traditional punishments common not only in post-war families. We had to put up with the reality of a man without inhibitions. Father, the secret warrior. That was the Stasi principle in those years.

And Robby, who was lying on the other side of the hall. He was moaning. He couldn't lift his head anymore, because his little body had banged against the wall. Repeatedly. I wanted to protect my brother. I wanted to do something, but I couldn't. I had been before him. Robby and I were father's dummies, his training objects, for years. I don't want to dwell on it. I don't want to write more than is necessary. It's hard, it hurts, but it has to be told here. Here and now. What happened then can't be shifted anywhere else. It has to be said right here, at this point. It happened and can't be argued away. Not by anything. It's still here and won't go away, can't go away. It remains, it persists, it has to stay here. Where else can it go? The words must return to this hallway. I don't want to describe or elaborate. I just want to make it clear that it actually existed. It took place. Our childhood was a childhood of terror. It has to be said. Otherwise it can't be understood. Otherwise what happened to Robby and me can't be understood. And what came afterwards can't be understood either. Violence changes everything. It gets into you and you become a different person. Father left the scene. He went to the toilet. He'd had enough for now. I wanted to reach out to my brother. I had to know how he was. He needed to know that I was there. I wanted to protect him. He stretched out his little hand to me. Our fingertips touched. That's all, we couldn't manage anything more. But it was enough. We were there, we had each other. We remained lying in the hallway. I listened to Robby breathing.

REPRESENTATIVE. There were lots of rooms in this apartment, lots of scenes, endless procedures, for at least four years, but that's not what it's about. 'To take something seriously means to be concrete ... because it is real.' Taking seriously the crack that opened up from then on in our childhood. It hadn't been great before, but this was in a different category, a different state. I lay there and wanted just to go back to the time before the hurt that Robby and I now carried inside, each of us in our own way. The hurt that would stay with us, even after we were no longer children and became other people. I heard father coming out of the toilet and going down the hall. In the kitchen he took a beer out of the fridge and sat down at the table to study the newspaper. When he passed us in the hall, we were lying on the floor, but he took no notice of us. He must have seen us, but he ignored us. The situation had escalated, it had got out of hand and then returned to normal. In other words, nothing had happened. Just another evening in December 1973 in a spacious apartment in the Weisser Hirsch. The air was the same, the floor was the same, the wall next to me was the same. Nothing had happened. But we had changed.

Grandfather, father and Robby. The search for my brother goes into the next round. More exactly it starts again here. Every sentence a testimony. And nothing will yield or go away. Because of Robby and because of the gondolas and because of the time and because of the East. Yes, I know, I can already hear it: how terrible. But it can't have been as bad as all that. And how was it possible? Who hadn't been paying attention? What a father! – And what about the mother? Where was she? – Don't worry, I'll get to her. Later. – But that's not what matters, that can't be what matters. I should make it clear that it wasn't an isolated case. The man without inhibitions is not alone. He is a representative, no more and no less. It's possible that this family was extreme, but extremism is also a reality. And it's part of the whole picture. Of course, I know that there were loving and protective parents in East Germany, but there were also lots of others. This is what the secret service, GDR police and military dossiers in the archives say. This is what psychologists and psychiatrists say about East Germany, pointing to the significantly high percentage of multiple neglect. This is what the protagonists of both generations who came after the young activists, the builders, the young Nazis, say. In the closed world of the 1970s, this generation passed on the pressure internally, in their families. Where else?

We are familiar with the idea of terror as the spectacular occupation of public space. The GDR in the 1970s experienced the acuteness internally, through a spectacular occupation in a quiet but effective manner of the interior space. The GDR of the 1970s was a country of repeat scenarios. The insidious Nazi education ideology drummed into the war children throughout the 1950s and 1960s, completely unprocessed and remote from reality, now broke free and was unleashed inwardly in the form of violence and helpless children. The enemy in the West was less of a threat in that regard than the population's own children. They were 'needed and abused so that the old ideals and attitudes could be maintained and not fall victim to devaluation and depression', wrote German psychoanalyst Werner Bohleber in 1994 about defence mechanisms in the families of perpetrators, fellow travellers and bystanders of the Nazi period. According to the National Socialist idea of upbringing, an emotional relationship to the child should be avoided at all costs; children should merely be provided for and controlled. Raising children was not about the child's own personality and needs, but about care, obedience and subordination with the aim of producing toughened, functional and well-nurtured children.

The social scientist and therapist Jan Lohl wrote in *Unbewusste Erbschaften des Nationalsozialismus*: 'Following the principles of Nazi education ideology, parents found it easier to see, treat and discipline the child as the bearer of their own feelings of inferiority, guilt and shame. According to Judith Kestenberg, the family situation in which these children grew up was often filled with the "aura of infanticide". These children often felt the hate and coldness of their parents that had been acted out destructively in National Socialist society or articulated by looking away.'

TWO FACES. I heard father turning the pages of the news-paper in the kitchen, then getting up to fetch another beer from the fridge. I heard him blow his nose, drink and put the bottle down. He knew that we were still lying in the hall. We couldn't get away. He saw and knew about everything. That's what he'd been trained for. One part of him was in Stuttgart, the second in Chemnitz, and the third at the kitchen table. His body went beyond the borders that closed off an entire country. The hallway was the least problem. 'Experiences are essentially not communicable,' said the writer and GDR dis-sident Reiner Kunze. That may be, but that's all we have. Just that, just us.

Father, who at some point turned off the light in the kitchen, went down the hall and stumbled into bed. What was the matter with this man? What was the matter with the members of the post-war generation after 1968, who were taken in by the system, who had allowed themselves to be called upon, who during the 'up and down of the GDR' had studied, pursued careers, built houses and founded families? Who couldn't get out, but also couldn't go forwards anymore, nor upwards, at best further downwards. The climate in East Germany in the 1970s: phantasm, and staging and suggestion as the two faces of the GDR as it entered its third decade, legitimized for a second time when Honecker took office, and even recognized worldwide. To the outside world it appeared more colourful, but internally the party and secret service were constructing a modern dictatorship. It was to be silent, indirect, hidden, unnoticed but at the same time targeted and hard. Mountains of files show that the Stasi in this time had extensive knowledge of the 'pathological normality' in this country, of the effects of its own repressive system, of the burden of National Socialism within families, of the particular preferences of those observed by it. It was knowledge that could be targeted to hold the population in check.

It must have been a ghostly atmosphere. A new authority that was in fact the same as the old one. One of gerontocrats, hardliners, ideologists and Cold War advocates, whom the post-war generation had no trust in. The Moscow clique had summoned them once and used them to install their own system. When it had become established, for them it was the end of the road, a dead end. With few exceptions, there was no way up. Life on a disused track. It was a time of disenchantment, disillusionment, also fear. But why was there never a political patricide, the revolt of the younger ones against the ossified political leaders? In that case, Hitler's children would have to have revolted against the victims of National Socialism. And that was the insurmountable inner barrier. An absolute taboo. The elders had ensured that this was the case. The Wall, the blockage, the limit was called Buchenwald. It bit and held as the political epidermis, a myth made of concrete that no one dared to push over. What happens in an enclosed system when the pressure cannot escape to the outside but also not upwards?

Klaus Theweleit's book *Männerfantasien* [published in German in 1977 and later translated into English as *Male Fantasies*], described National Socialism as the practical expression of catastrophic physical states. As a dangerous material that through power and violence forces the state of a person's own body to match the state of the world. And father? A man without inhibitions who was subsumed in the countless identities, who had to reinvent himself, because of the borders, the outline, his own powerlessness. Who ritually activated this unbounded state through his excesses so as to find relief for himself in it and maybe in this way to escape from it.

I want the crack to remain a crack and the internal wound not to heal. I want to get rid of the ice pick, I want to be Robby's witness, the only one, the last one. And yet we both also observed how endlessly father suffered. You can't be a terrorist forever. Every long-term terrorist at some point has a problem. Father had flaky skin. All over. Bloody, open lesions on his head, his elbows, his back and his chest. When he came home from his courses, it was time for another series of cream pots beside the washbasin. He took stinking dark brown baths, leaving a dark brown rim in the tub. Our towels became dark brown, as did the bathroom mat. But the more baths my father took and the more cream he put on, the more he tried to beat himself to death through us, the more acute it became. It was so acute that I sometimes thought you could look right into his soul through these lesions. The matt flakes of dry skin that he shed from his body and that just returned with renewed force spread all over the apartment like tallow, dull snow.

IN THE DARKROOM. I think of Robby, who while studying art in the mid-1990s, tried to look over the neighbour's fence and find a backdoor to get back to our childhood, really to break into it. He was getting on for thirty at the time, lost in his memories, and wanted to find the back way to our place. In his work diary he wrote: 'I try to look through our old letter slot and discover that the flap has just been unscrewed and turned round. So we are still there, because on the back is our surname. A gap of twelve years bridged in this way. I took advantage of the sun to take photos in the courtyard, a sad building. Probably not much use without a comment. But for me it's vital. Confusion again.'

Robby's confusion and the phantom dolls again. 'I took photos of toys that I recently got hold of,' he wrote, 'for example my old doll. I took close-up photos of the objects and created a relationship to myself by lying next to them. I called the cycle memory pattern. When I look at the pictures of myself, I am shocked to see how present the thought of death is. Once again, Roland Barthes' explanation: "The only thought I can have is that at the end of this first death, my own death is inscribed."'

Robby's nearness to death. The doll, which is the other witness. Which sees nothing but has seen everything. It won't reveal it. It can't. At best it can provide indications. And it can conceal. It is close, but not too close. It is a body, but not your body. It is an illusion and your childhood. Dolls are easy targets. My brother's head next to the shiny pink doll. An image and a doorway into a time that he himself doesn't remember. He seeks, sets off on a trail, tries to construct it with the aid of photos. What can be made of a childhood that passes from a toy doll to a combat training dummy? What can be seen with eyes that can't see? Is a world clearer if you try to say something without words? Robby believed this. That's what he believed in, in mental films, not in mental words. He didn't want to be hurt again. 'Everyone has his own mental darkroom,' he wrote in his work diary.

I think of surrealistic films, of Buñuel and Bellmer, but above all of Cindy Sherman and her defiant, inflammatory images. Her wide eyes, her face that bursts from the inside. Always the same face, the same ravaged body. Wounds, abiding landscapes, nightmares. Strikingly beautiful, aestheticized, as if a smooth protective skin had been placed over everything, as if there were a place but no place. How is it that the pictures don't just disintegrate when you look at them? I think of the blurring and confusion I feel immediately when I confront her images. Of the nakedness, the exposure, the threat, as if someone had taken hold of my breathing, as if her dolls were staring at me from the picture. I think of Robby, perhaps seeking his gaze. Words are needed, other ones, stronger, clearer.

A DAY AT THE POOL

Bühlau open-air swimming pool – the summer institution of our childhood. It is a memory of glances, first kisses, being pushed off the three-metre board, chlorine, back floating and the noise of voices. I disappear into a wooden changing cabin. Robby takes the one next to me. Ready? he pesters me through the wooden boards. He's nervous. Nowhere is it so clear that we are six years apart. He doesn't like that at all. But Bühlau is where we hang out, Bühlau has to be, Bühlau is about bodies.

I come out of the cabin wearing a red bikini. I don't have any breasts to speak of, but my legs are quite long. Robby has a sky-blue rubber ring around his waist and is wearing a diving mask. My brother loves equipment. He needs it. Let's go, I shout. We run across the vast sunbathing area, stuff our clothes underneath our blanket, and dive into the turquoise water. It sparkles and bubbles. The light looks like water, the water like light. Something dazzles us. The water, the sun, a mirror, the promise in the air? The chlorine stings our eyes. We splash each other, swallow litres of water, laugh. My brother wants to show me his first head-first dive. With a rubber ring. The boys at the side of the pool hoot with laughter. I tap my forehead at them. But Robby has already had enough, blue lips, hunger. We flop onto the blanket. Close your eyes and tell me a story with a happy ending, I say. No such thing, asserts Robby.

What we have is sandwiches, crackers, biscuits and endless sun. Our bodies sweat, the blades of grass prick us through the blanket, a trail of ants runs over my brother's foot, we observe the people hanging around the sunbathing area. The beautiful tall trees, the pool attendant's whistle that can speak. Two short shrill blasts means get out. One long staccato burst: get out immediately.

And then: Look who's coming, whispers Robby to me. It's Stefan, two classes above me. I'd long spotted him, of course. It's because of him that I'm here. Do you want to go for a swim with me? he asks. I gaze at Stefan up and down and look right, to my brother. He shakes his head. I look at Stefan and shake my head. He turns around and leaves. Why not? I ask Robby when we are alone again. It's better with the two of us, he says. That sounds final.

Country within a country

DENSE GREY. When I was fourteen I was sent to boarding school. That was 1974. My departure coincided with father starting work as an agent. Wickersdorf special school was in the deepest Thuringian Forest near Saalfeld. It was founded in 1906 as an independent school community by Gustav Wyneken, Walter Benjamin's teacher, and soon became the symbol of the German youth movement. The reform education movement here came to an end in 1933. The GDR also rejected the progressive education concept and called the teachers who still felt committed to the founding idea 'anarchist pseudo-revolutionaries'. They were disciplined, suspended, arrested. Wickersdorf was aligned to the prevailing ideology and in 1964 it became one of the two special schools for Russian in the GDR. Before long it was dubbed the 'red cadre smithy'.

A landscape afflicted by the warm, dry föhn, the keen bite of the wind, the clanging of the school bell. We gathered for assembly, stood in rows of three, listened to the principal's address, the flags fluttered. It was all the same everywhere, regardless of the school: assemblies, flags, oaths, empty words. White blouses, blue blouses, red neckerchiefs, blue neckerchiefs. We stood in rank and file. The principal worked for the foreign secret service, the class teacher was the institute's main informer, the school itself had a mentoring agreement with the Stasi. I didn't want to be there. I suffered from having been thrown out of the family. Yet it was my salvation. Wickersdorf – a place for an idea. For something that was to become inescapable and weighed heavily on the mind. Like a residual world in which the only possibility was to try to get by.

Through running, for example. That became my main activity. As soon as classes were over, I would climb the steps, leave the school grounds, glance back over the dense greyness of the village and stand at the top of the hill at the edge of the fields with nothing but sky above. Nothing else, I didn't need anything else. It was beautiful. I thought of Robby and how much I missed him. What was he up to? Mother sent a letter with a photo of him. With his home-made Indian headdress holding a yellow plastic tomahawk. Proud and beaming. Your brother is a joy to us, she wrote on the back. But how was he really? I was on the outside, that was clear. Something had come to an end. There were no procedures anymore. At least I hoped so. But Robby?

The magic of running. I flew away, waiting for the moment of transition, became light, disembodied, transformed into a state I can't describe. Why should I? It belonged to me. I had found something for myself. Something where I was alone, invulnerable and unreachable. I just had to run. Then it came of its own accord. I had only to reach this point in me and let go. It knew more than me. I could rely on it. It had something to do with willpower. It had to get out. The main thing was not to hold back but to get away. That's what it was about. I had become a refugee who had to get out of myself, who just wanted to get away and leave myself behind. A situation, energy, pain. At the same time, I had no idea of the real change that had taken place in my life.

DIGGING IN. In 1976, the poet Reiner Kunze was banned from working because of his book *Die wunderbaren Jahre*. That same year, the songwriter Wolf Biermann was deprived of his GDR citizenship, an act that was to rebound on the Honecker crew. Biermann – the litmus test for the pseudo-liberal GDR. Everyone was required to show their colours, and polls were held in practically every work brigade. A yes for Biermann meant a no to socialism. A no could mean arrest, interrogation, expulsion from college, dismissal. 'Time was sleepless,' wrote the poet Gabriele Stötzer. 'We were trapped in a witches' cauldron, with our fears in the GDR brew.'

In 1979, the law got tougher on political crimes, particularly regarding freedom of speech. And with it the ceaseless talk of work in progress, stage wins, the historically unique claims of socialism, which had simply become annoying. The political rewriting in the decades before, Buchenwald as the historical seal and central falsification of history, the formation of a 'socialist state consciousness' – all this had created a reality with deep cracks right down to the foundations. People lived in a small world on hold that was perhaps a little more colourful but had ultimately become very quiet. No more celebration, no more parades as in the early years, and if so then only stage-managed ones. Whatever was going on, it was concealed from view. Hidden, indirect, inauthentic. A school of concealment, fear, lies, of private withdrawal and inward-looking points of reference, in which the GDR attempted to disconnect from the world but also from the silence about the early years of terror. It was a time of digging in.

That's what happened, I like to say. That's how it was. But to assert this, I should have kept a clear record of it all at the time. Not only what we talked about or what the country talked of, thought and felt, but also how we lived, what we ate, the clothes we wore and the foibles we had. But it wasn't possible. I was at school, ran nonstop through the countryside, lay at night under a blanket and listened for the first time to radio from the West. That hadn't been possible in Dresden. There people lived on another planet. But Wickersdorf was at the edge of the country, near the border to Franconia. With a bit of luck, Bruce Springsteen would roar out 'Born to Run' for me again under the bedclothes. Bruce Springsteen had better things to do, but beyond our school, beyond the forest, there had to be something else. Another world. We all realized that at least. The school – an area with slate-coloured buildings with combative names. 'Red October', 'Partisan', 'Young Guard', 'Sunburst'. If I recall correctly, we lived in 'Red Star'. The school principal lived on the ground floor. His voice crept up as far as our rooms. A voice that reminded me of my father.

Returning home to Dresden, every six to eight weeks. I travelled to see Robby, who had no time. He sat in grandfather's armchair in front of the television and watched *Chingachgook, die Grosse Schlange*, one of twelve films that turned the world of the Red Indians of East Germany into a country within the country. My brother had spears to ram into the ground, he had to ward off the fiercest attacks, look far into the distance, save his people, lead them across the river, chase the baddies and suffer at the stake, before riding off into the sunset with the beautiful Wahtawah. An Indian doesn't speak, he acts. He greeted me, swung his yellow plastic tomahawk and referred to me thereafter as either Running Elk or Split Oak.

RE-ENACTMENT. The country within a country. The German studies scholar Katharina Grabbe exposed in *Das Imaginäre der Nation* the enormous scope for identification offered by the DEFA Westerns, shot after 1966 following the 'Kaninchenfilme'[1] or the banning of an entire year's worth of DEFA production. Films that were meant to paste over the void left by the devastating ban and convincingly demonstrate the depoliticization of the film industry. But East German Red

[1] Films that were banned without public screening.

Indians? What was that about? Essentially, it was the story of a re-enactment. 'Lightly clothed in leather breeches and fringed shirt, with a feather in his flowing black hair and war paint on his noble face, from the nineteenth century at the latest the Indian made his fleet-footed entry – in moccasins, needless to say – into the collective German imagination and helped to shape it,' writes Grabbe. Founded in 1946 with the aim of cranking up the huge fantasy machine evoking the better Germany, DEFA and its films instrumentalized the Karl May productions that had been appearing in the West since 1962 and above all the huge popularity they enjoyed. Could this theme be useful to us as well?

The first in the series of GDR Westerns, *Die Söhne der Grossen Bärin*, released in 1966, was a massive box office hit, attracting almost ten million spectators. The country was gripped by an Indian fever that the authorities knew how to inflame even further. In the 1970s, Christmas wasn't complete without one of these blockbuster films on the television. In the 1980s, a real Indian scene developed, with its own culture and communities, which saw themselves as an eco-romantic alternative to the official way of life. But what was behind this Indian hype? The screenplay for the model Indian saw him as an innocent victim of capitalist intrigue and colonial politics that was interested solely in power, land and profits. The honest redskin was surrounded, fought to the last, starved, had modest desires, loved nature, tamed the buffalo and was loyal to his brothers. He was the incarnation of reason, with its virtuous catalogue in support of the free untamed land of socialist Protestantism, exploiting the immense desire of the East Germans to be allowed to be good without the burden of history.

In this amalgamated Indian hero, the Buchenwald myth was re-potted and re-enacted with the aid of a more universal plot. In that sense it is the contemporary, depoliticized variant of the myth. Ulbricht needed red anti-fascism as a national ideology to bring the East German people into line. Honecker needed the Red Indian as a noble partisan, as it were, to establish the GDR as a nation in the long term. Right after the war, the Buchenwald myth had a powerful unburdening effect, particularly for the war children. In its rewriting, the wide-open spaces of unattainable America fired the imagination of the huge generation of war grandchildren, the baby boomers of East Germany. The country itself was hermetically sealed, but in the mythical land of red-skinned fraternity, the children of the Wall were able to deal with the inherited guilt of their parents' and grandparents' generation, at least temporarily.

The DEFA Western films were made between 1965 and 1985 and shown throughout most of Eastern Europe. Genuine long-running bestsellers. These films also brought Robby to Karl May, who had lived in Radebeul, a suburb of Dresden. The Karl May Museum there was rebranded in 1956 as an Indian museum. The author himself was not included in the definitive canon of GDR state literature. He and his books were taboo. He was not banned, but he was not welcome either. His fan community, his aura, was all the more powerful as a result, particularly in Saxony. How often did I stand with my brother in front of the glass show windows in Radebeul. To admire the colourful headdresses, the sumptuous accessories of a remote, exotic world, everything, of course, invented by Karl May specially for Robby. What did he find so fascinating about him? Perhaps he represented a means of finding a good father. One whom he never had to meet and was therefore not threatening. One who had written books that my brother adored, although he wasn't allowed to read them and didn't know them. In East Germany only scattered private remnants existed. Robby's dream of a Winnetou book remained unfulfilled until 1983. Then the GDR relented and published the long-forbidden author.

The two of us took the tram home from Radebeul. We were silent. How are you doing? I asked, in the hope that Robby would tell me about himself. Are you OK? He glanced at me, rubbed his eye, pushed back his hair and said finally: Crazy Horse's real name is Tȟašúŋke Witkó. He was the chief of one of the Oglala tribes belonging to the Western Sioux. Okay, I said. He didn't want to talk. Did he resent it that I was away? No, it wasn't that. Robby and I had been in a place we didn't want to be reminded of. Not now. Not like this. We didn't understand it. We had no words for it. We withdrew. We were embarrassed by one another. It was difficult.

My brother had erected his wigwam in the courtyard. When we got home, we made a fire. I fetched wood from the shed. We stuck potatoes on sticks and placed them in the flames. After a while he said: There's trouble. – What is it? – Two kids from my class painted swastikas in the school toilets. Now all hell has broken loose. One announcement after the other. They want to know who did it. – And? – No idea. I wasn't there. But now we have to clean the toilets all the time. He turned his potato. The fire crackled. We stared at the flames. When was that? I can't remember exactly. 1979 or 1980, I think. I must have already been at the sports club in Jena. It was the first time I heard about the swastikas.

INNER MEANING. The story of the East and its antisemitism after 1945. Archives as early as 1947 document the desecration of the Jewish cemetery in Chemnitz and the destruction of another cemetery in Zittau. Incidents that continued, accumulated, increased steadily. The authorities made sure that the public knew nothing about them. In 1959, a polytechnic in Chemnitz, renamed Karl-Marx-Stadt in 1953, was smeared with swastikas. There was a strikingly large and persistent number of such incidents in Saxony. According to an unpublished analysis by the youth organization FDJ, thirty-two schools in Dresden district saw 'fascist provocations' in 1966. Pupils from Dresden-Ost, Pirna, Freital and Görlitz used Nazi slogans and symbols. Nearly ten years later, a second analysis noted that 'the number of neo-fascist incidents has increased'.

Before the Holocaust there were around 85,000 Jews living in the east of Germany. According to a 1946 census in the Soviet occupied zone, there were still 4,500 practising Jews. A survey of the Jewish communities in 1951 revealed that 1,244 members remained. In 1975 there were 813, a year later 710. The reason for the departure of the few lingering Jews also needs to be stated. It is about Stalin's anti-Jewish paranoia and the political antisemitism of the Ulbricht clan. The figures also indicate that the burgeoning neo-Nazi scene in East Germany managed to exist practically without any Jews living there.

The GDR's policy of forgetting has two major flaws: on the one hand the 'inability to mourn', and on the other the deliberate impediment to mourning. By its third decade, the concretized memory of GDR anti-fascism had become so brittle that the Wall generation in particular no longer believed the regime's stories of the great victory and the fuss about the erstwhile claim to a historical legacy. How can living in a cage be seen as a victory? The war grandchildren began to rattle the bars but didn't break them. Why not? Why again no political patricide? The societal glue still held, but above all it was the 'internalized sense of the parental line of defence', as the social psychologist Michael Buchholz wrote in his essay 'The unconscious transference between the generations'. But the harsh derealization of the past during the first major rewrite after the war began to weigh heavily. In the static internal climate of East Germany, the Nazi history that was supposed to have been dealt with and outsourced to the West turned into a revenant of a special kind.

This was particularly true of Hitler's grandchildren, who had the political task of making Communism a reality. They were the torch bearers of a red future, except that no one had asked them about it. Being transported to the open spaces of the Wild West was one thing, putting up with the bigoted reality was another. The enclosed generation, the Wall children in particular, were the direct recipients of the interminable droning about 'nation, heimat, fatherland'. Honecker's mobilization programme was meant to stop the internal erosion of the regime. The message to those born afterwards was of 'unreserved love, respect and above all defence' of the GDR nation. In 1978, 'military education' as a premilitary class was introduced as a compulsory subject for all pupils in years 9 and 10.

On the one hand the slipping away, the false bottom, the clock stopped, the drill, the spoon-feeding, the authority, the immutability of the GDR, on the other hand the ceaseless propaganda charge. And then also family secrets, the total silence, the violence, the denial by the parent generation. The resistance grew. The young sought radicalization, differentiation, detachment. It was a matter of fundamental opposition. Angry, vulnerable young people with Mohican haircuts, tattered clothes, dog chains around their necks, lace-up boots, tattoos. It was immediately evident that the East German punks in the 1980s were the start of a scene that completely rejected the system and that couldn't be so easily silenced. They were too stark, too hard-headed, too tough. 'It was also somehow cool,' said a punk from Leipzig, 'when we would go through the town in a group and the normal zonies[2] would shout after us: "Put them all in concentration camps!" I liked it when we made them show their true face.'

Stasi boss Mielke once again put a stop to it all. The youthful protest was quashed. Calling them 'degenerate, asocial, controlled by the West', he found a way of criminalizing the East German punks. The first generation was deliberately isolated, its leaders arrested, conscripted into the army or deported to the West. Of seventeen punk bands, six were disbanded and their members imprisoned. The alert and raging punks could

[2] Residents of the former Russian zone, which was to become the GDR.

have spoken for an entire generation had they not been ground down from the beginning.

In the Stasi situation reports, it was the left-wing punks who attracted most attention. For a long time, the Stasi ignored the right-wing skinhead groups, their plans, recruitment and organization. It described them as 'negative decadent' youths and classed them in general as imported from and seduced by the West. The long pent-up racism and increasing fascistization of East Germany were not allowed to feature in the plans and were hushed up and kept secret. In May 1988, a court case opened in Oranienburg against a group of skinheads who had been arrested after going on a violent rampage at a dance. Offences before 1988 were also mentioned. The court estimated that the youths would not have behaved as they did 'if it hadn't been for the RIAS[3] in Berlin,' wrote the historian Harry Waibel in his book about antisemitism and neo-Nazism in the GDR. His study provides a wealth of material about the tactical links between the Stasi and left- and right-wing terrorism, the neo-Nazi scene in the National People's Army, the Volkspolizei, the border guards and structural violence in the GDR.

There were quite often family connections between the skinheads and the Stasi, with frequent cases of aggression and criminal offences being covered up by the perpetrators' own fathers in the Ministry for State Security. They confirmed the work discipline of this rearguard and found it comforting that 'the vast majority of skinheads do not refuse to perform their military service. They see military training as part of their "Germanness",' surmised a Stasi colonel. It was at once an oath of disclosure and a description of the situation. Something here was being deliberately hushed up.

The formation in the early 1980s of militant neo-Nazi gangs such as Wotan's Brothers in Halberstadt, the Lichtenberg

[3] Rundfunk im amerikanischen Sektor [Radio in the American Sector]: a radio and television station in West Berlin.

Front in East Berlin, the NS-Kradstaffel Friedrichshain, the SS-Division Wolgast and the Weimar Front was accompanied by bomb attacks, swastika daubing, brutal assaults and the attempted murder of foreigners. The Stasi knew that at the end of the 1980s there were three to four times as many skinheads in the East as in the West. The movement had not only taken off but had become brutal and more targeted. 'At the end of 1989, 5,000 neo-Nazis under the black, white and red Reich flag formed the militant, ideological hard core of the radical right-wing movement,' wrote Waibel. With them were around 10,000 neo-Nazi sympathizers.

CAPE OF GOOD HOPE

Greenland, shouts my brother, Greenland first. – No, the Golden Gate Bridge, I offer. Better the Bosporus first. – Let's go to the Bermuda Triangle. Places, landscapes that we have to see. It's a game that Robby and I play when we occupy – or more precisely enter – an empty villa. My brother usually knows the people in the Weisser Hirsch district who have emigrated to the West. They are friends, neighbours, fellow pupils. There is always a certain interregnum between the old and new tenants. The key for the abandoned house is underneath one of the large clay bowls in the garden. It's quite simple. From the back entrance into the hall, to the right the kitchen, another hallway and then onwards. Every room a new city, a new country. Easter Island, asserts Robby. No, Paris. – More like Colmar. – Madagascar, I say, but only because I like the name so much. No idea where it might be.

How often do the occupants take a last look at the familiar setting, then close the doors behind them, cut the cord and finally tear away. Who goes? Who stays? Who is inside, who is outside? And then? What does a break of this nature in their own lives signify? Where do they end up? What do they leave behind? Did I ever ask myself that? On the parquet floor in the spacious dining room the traces of the furniture that has also left. And marks everywhere else as well, the pictures that used to hang on the walls, the last fire in the fireplace. In the attic the creaking of wood, spiders' webs, dust, flies. So loud that it sounds as if old voices have gathered there for a last conversation. Three wrinkled apples on a windowsill. Last news from an abandoned country.

In front of the entrances are putti, in the garden abandoned children's toys. The villas are huge. We don't want to steal or destroy anything. We just want to open the doors and imagine what the life inside used to be like. Steps, odours, light and shadow, long journeys. Sometimes we loiter, sometimes we run up the long staircases, sometimes we simply stop and ask what the houses have started to be silent about. We forget that we shouldn't be here. In the meantime the empty rooms belong to us.

Gaps in time

WAITING ROOMS. One might have assumed that after Hitler, Germany would have collapsed mentally and slid into a deep collective depression. None of this happened, neither in East nor in West Germany. Jan Lohl pointed out instead in *Unbewusste Erbschaften des Nationalsozialismus* that in both post-fascist societies, perpetrators, fellow travellers and spectators, the majority of Germans, unconsciously built a crypt, a kind of altar of the soul, so as to maintain the grandiose self-image that had been created in the Nazi period. If it weren't for this inflated self, collapse threatened. 'The lost narcissistic object was incorporated and detached' in an enclosed space in the heart of the ego, functioning there as a stabilizing force. It was also a guarantee for the promised return to normality. In reality, this inner German crypt was probably nothing other than the indirect admission of the dimension of the country's guilt. It not only averted the 'desire to avoid a narcissistic crisis' (unpleasure) and the responsibility, but also maintained the 'imaginary link to the object'.

The revenant dwelling inside had its great moment in the West in 1970 when the Red Army Faction sent it after the leaders of the state. At its core a diversionary tactic aimed once again at working around the lines of defence in the heavily burdened West German families. If they had sounded out their own origins at close quarters, it could have undermined the already fragile defence of the post-war generation. There were sufficient public archives and tracing services in the Federal Republic to fill out the taboos and holes in family biographies – like the Wehrmachtsauskunftsstelle für Kriegerverluste und Kriegsgefangene[1] in Berlin. Millions of file cards as memory of the army.

By the same token, the Red Cross tracing service in Munich, with its 50 million file cards, could be seen as the memory of the missing and the destiny of loss. There was also the memory of those killed in action in the form of the Volksbund Deutscher Kriegsgräberfürsorge, the German war graves commission. By 1989 it had documented 2.5 million dead in 825 war cemeteries. With the collapse of the Eastern Bloc a further three million dead were added.

Hitler's war mania had torn eighteen million German men from their civilian lives. Over five million died in his army and turned Germany until 1956 into one huge waiting room. There were candles in the windows, plates on the table waiting for the missing family members finally to return. People in both East and West Germany hoped and prayed. Access to the archives became the basis and point of reference for the family memory. A silent, permanent and at all events well organized source of reliable information – albeit confined to the West.

INTERMINABLE. There was no army information service or war graves commission in the GDR. The National Day of Mourning was not an official day of commemoration. There were no separate military cemeteries or central memorials. According to the political scientist Tobias Voigt, one of the

[1] Army Information Service for Missing Persons and Prisoners of War – WASt.

main exceptions was the Halbe military cemetery. There was a Protestant clergyman there who, from 1946, sought to recover and bury the many dead in the surrounding forests. Halbe is therefore probably the only large memorial in the GDR to German soldiers killed in the Second World War. In Oderbruch, the grave of a single soldier, still visited regularly today, stands for thousands of other casualties of war.

Those seeking information about the whereabouts of fathers, brothers, uncles or grandfathers had to obtain it from the West by making an inquiry with the Red Cross. Many East Germans knew nothing about it. The prospects were uncertain. The mail was monitored. Those who had relatives in the West had to rely on them and were able to make inquiries through them. An icy silence prevailed regarding those who were still in Russian captivity or Gulags after 1945 and why they were still there. Stalin kept the prisoners as political collateral and maintained a macabre and deliberate confusion about them. The less clear and more divergent the information about the number of captives, the greater the pressure and the room for negotiation with the Germans. A total of 1.3 million German soldiers died in Soviet captivity. After Adenauer's visit to Moscow in September 1955, 10,000 soldiers and twice the number of civilian captives returned to Germany. The last train arrived in mid-January 1956.

The GDR regarded information about the situation of the Germans stuck in the Soviet Union as being without substance. In the official narrative, in the media and in schools the detainees were seen as war criminals. There is no doubt that some of them were precisely that, but they made up only 10 per cent at most. The vast majority of those who disappeared over the years in the Nirvana of the giant Soviet empire received arbitrarily severe sentences, sometimes up to twenty-five years' confinement. Many were arrested, shot or sentenced after 1945 by the NKVD, the Soviet secret police, as political opponents. When the survivors from this group returned to

East Germany in winter 1956, people said that there must have been a reason why they were away so long. They were held in suspicion and were considered lawbreakers in the eyes of the new state authorities. As long as the GDR existed, the late returnees formed no part of the public memory.

What does it do to a society when the wartime fates of grandfathers, brothers, uncles and fathers remain unexplained, and the early story of opposition in the GDR was rewritten as the story of enemies of state? When questions can't be asked, when feelings have no meaning, because they are not allowed to have one, when there is no way of escaping the totalitarian suppression? When do people stop hoping, waiting, thinking, asking? Where do they put the interminable sadness?

GENERATIONAL SYNAPSES. Memories have something unyielding about them. Sometimes they hurtle towards you like a hard unadorned dream. I remember our countless school outings to Soviet barracks, our badges, pennants, neckerchiefs, flowers, our words learned off by heart: We are proud. We swear allegiance. We are fighters for happiness. I remember huge, brightly lit rooms, smooth floors, tedious balalaika music, the anthems, the pathos, the soaring Russian melodies, the strangely overdramatized heroism of the whole thing, the smell of garlic wafting over the tables, but particularly our shaven-headed Soviet heroes. Young soldiers. We hurriedly pressed our flowers and pennants into their hands. In front of us were the saddest men in the world, with huge, burning eyes. How is it possible ever to get them out of our heads?

Perhaps these mental images that Robby sought so intensively exist in reality. At any event, something coalesces in me, as if in an imaginary vessel, internalized feelings in material form. I see hundreds of children standing helplessly before their heroes, handing over stamps, flowers and badges, thanking them and parroting heroic epic poems, as if they would like to do something so the childlike, alien soldiers did not have these bulging eyes. The life of these shaven-headed men that was even more encapsulated than ours.

In this image, which overlaps with many others, at some point we children go home. There we find our grandfathers, uncles, fathers, all of whom fought against the Soviet heroes and were now criminals, fascists, murderers. What does that do to families and with children who are not supported and stabilized by an authoritative narrative of mourning but have to make do with their parents' labyrinthine silence? What are they meant to feel and think when the state has forced their own family history to disappear forever in a fog created to make sure that it does not re-emerge? When there is no reliable memory?

The French psychoanalyst Nicolas Abraham explored the counterpart to the parental crypt and came up with the term 'phantom'. This is a necessary invention by the following generations, who need to give form, be it through hallucination, individually or collectively, to the void created in them through the blanking out of part of the life of a loved object. It is a kind of seismographic interpretation in the unconscious mind of the following generations of gaps in the family memory, silence, parental fears. 'Unconsciously, the children therefore have a very good idea,' writes Jan Lohl, 'of what their parents do not reveal of their life stories.' They are suspicious of the black holes in the family saga. Every gesture, every hesitation, every omission is gauged by their disturbed emotional scanner and translated into a toxic system. 'At the emotional level, the unconscious fantasies regarding the history of their own forebears are steeped in aggression and violence,' says Lohl.

The process is complicated. At its heart is a code of silence between parents and children designed to protect the family secret at all costs, however incriminating it might be. The more the generational synapses are put under strain, the more agile, encroaching, invasive the phantom of the generation born afterwards becomes. 'It aggressively guards the derealization of the parents' history and forms in them the family "aura of infanticide".' Lohl writes that many sons and daughters from perpetrator and fellow-traveller families live in fear that their parents would kill them if they revealed the family secret. Through this pact, family loyalty becomes a law of survival, a principle of suppression for the sake of their own lives. It means: say nothing, do nothing, so as not to disturb the false Holy Grail of peace in the family. The price is high, not only in private. Ultimately, it also determines the mood of a society.

But where does the private archive of mourning meet the public archive of memory? Do they meet? Yes. Do we need it? Yes. As an anchor, a fixed point, a possible focal point to achieve clarity, solid ground and inner distance through facts, documents and evidence. But the dislocated object of mourning is too big. I think of my second grandmother and how she looked forward to seeing me every day. How she took the photo of grandfather from the buffet and placed it on the table between her and me. How I automatically assumed his role and thought of questions to ask her to make her speak. I was the missing person who never returned. About whom nothing was known.

Looking back, I can only think that she invested all her hope in me. I was someone who simply turned up, ate a whole bag of cherries, looked for the thousandth time at the photos in the old Persil box and read aloud from the red book. We sat facing each other and admired the drawings in it. Grandmother said: 'scrofulous eye'. I saw a battered bloodshot thing that could be anything. A jellyfish, a huge diatom. On the next page were movement studies. Grandmother said what they were: 'myopathies'. I saw a naked woman who became more angular from picture to picture. In the end we saw a face cut into a mosaic, and on the next page a plate-sized crater in a stomach. Grandmother gently stroked the wounds in the book. She read what was written under one of the phantom pictures: 'Time

is the most important factor in the struggle for survival.' The
woman opposite me was looking for her husband. Did she keep
her hopes alive a bit longer through me?

ORIENTATIONS. The public denial of the fields of the dead
in the GDR and the private grief. The state myth of Buchenwald
and the East German collective war crypt. The GDR war children had contributed significantly to the rebuilding of the
state, but their mind's-eye images, recollections and hopes
were buried in the piles of inaccessible information. They were
unable to clear up anything. They lived possessed by the absent,
by the silence, by the borrowed feelings of guilt. On top of the
unprocessed National Socialism came a new indoctrination,
the unopposed demands of the regime or an active perpetrator
existence and hence the awareness of having become incriminated again in a second violent system. But the inarticulable
conflict between the war children and grandchildren was stuck
in time. Two generations watching one another and sealing
themselves off. The new generation was puzzled at the cobbled
together careers of their parents, the abstruse sentences with
which they chose to ignore the world crumbling around them.
The young sought affront, negation, rebuttal, but often enough
they didn't trust themselves. When the East German punks
and skinheads agitated in their deliberate opposition to the
system, they were crying out, a cry that was often accompanied
by a desire for extreme measures. State and private authority
were eroded. The phantom escaped and began to lash out. A
stalemate, which contributed significantly to the collapse of
the GDR. The writer Sylvia Kabus commented on the post-war
generation of the 1980s: 'This fear of the children growing up.
The icy shock at the idea that the younger generation did not
suffer the disfigurement that had been put up with for so long,
that it was not unavoidable and that it could have been done
differently. The ever-present violence that rises up through
fatalism and self-contempt.'

The country was writing its epilogue. The war grandchildren ran with absurd hairstyles and surreal clothes through streets that under normal circumstances would have been called a war landscape. The world about us was slipping, crumbling, rotting. How isolated, how detached we all lived in it! By this time I had become a sprinter, catapulted into the world, and expunged my inner turmoil by running in huge stadiums. In Cologne against Evelyn Ashford, in Bratislava against Jarmila Kratochvílová, in Rome against Merlene Ottey. Necessity can also help you to run fast. When I got back to Jena, where I was studying and training, there was Robby standing at the door. My brother, me, and our search for ourselves. Our roundabout routes. As if we were hunting in a soundproof room, without talking, with no escape. It was about intimate inquiry, about Beuys, Büchner and the Bauhaus.

The very first Beuys exhibition came to East Germany in early 1988 at the Akademie-Galerie in Berlin. Joseph Beuys, the sphinx, who had died two years previously. An endless line of people in front of the entrance. Robby and I went through the rooms. No word between us. We didn't prejudge, we didn't interpret, we observed and felt as if we had arrived at something that had meaning for us. The catalogue spoke of warmth, sound, plasticity. It was a question of healing. I don't think we understood it. We stumbled on. *Monument to the Stag, The Pack, Genghis Khan, Exploding Skull with Metal, Waterfalls, Man in Stone, Point Where a Fairy Tale Happened.* Beuys' titles were like landmarks, orientations. The exhibition a sketch, a breath, something unfocused. As was mostly the case in East Germany, there was something to see that was not marginal but also not essential, not the centre. We saw and we didn't see. But for us it was an echo chamber. 'Biography is more than just a purely personal matter,' wrote Beuys.

In the Kunsthalle Weimar just a few weeks later, the major Büchner exhibition that had been shown a year earlier on the Mathildenhöhe in Darmstadt. Büchner compact. Robby and I hitchhiked from Jena on the highway. On the right on the high ground was where Napoleon fought in 1806, an event that is stuck firmly in my head. Why? Shortly before Weimar the view across the countryside with Buchenwald on the horizon. The tower as an ironclad symbol. Lots of young people in front of the Kunsthalle in the city of Goethe's birth, lots of students, who had joined Büchner on his revolutionary trip. The language, the socializing, the drama, the nerves. My brother and I drifted for hours through the anatomy of an era. The attentiveness to the material. How it is peeled off, how it is discussed from all points of view, how the details organize the regard. The story tells of unpacked, undisguised micro-vectors. A completely different way of thinking. The intellectual as scalpel. This was new to us. Non-ideological investigation of perception through images and language, excavated by an East-West German research team. The gravitational force was provided by the West. The thought revolution came from there. Büchner tormented and illuminated. I remember hundreds of bodies. Bodies like those in grandmother's red book. I remember Büchner's Darmstadt as an imaginary space. Eighteen months later I was living there.

And finally Konrad Wachsmann, the legendary Bauhaus architect, who flew in from the USA in the final phase of the GDR. His *Wachsmann Report* was published in 1986 and was one of those books that brought East Germany back to the present day. We read and internalized it as if someone had given the order to excavate Atlantis. As early as the end of the 1940s, aesthetic Modernism had already been outlawed in the east of Germany.

Everything that could come under the heading 'bourgeois decadence' was eradicated. The attacks on the intellect were organized, brutal and extremely effective. Looking back, the extent of the hollowing out is hard to imagine and yet it was quite clear. Alfred Kurella, the culture ideologist of the early GDR said in the late 1950s: 'Artists in our camp should suffer and be indignant at pictures by Miró, music by Nono, books by Joyce, Beckett or Tennessee Williams.' Picasso, the man with the dove of peace, was for him a 'gigantic ruin', who was 'crushed under the spell of decadent artistic activity'.

The intellectual crisis in the East and its decades of disconnection from modern Europe – from its aesthetic and memory processes – created a climate that brutally shifted the horizon of acceptance of East German society. Konrad Wachsmann, born in 1901 in Frankfurt/Oder, restored a sense of proportion. He is the cultural history of the twentieth century par excellence. Jew and exile, cosmopolitan and whiskey lover. He studied in Hellerau near Tessenow and was a master student of Poelzig. Konrad Wachsmann built for Einstein and met them all: Kokoschka in Dresden, Brecht in Berlin, Le Corbusier in Paris, Feininger in New York, Gropius in Lincoln, Massachusetts. A man of the century, who brought together the Bauhaus in Weimar and the Bauhaus in Chicago. A docking system.

What Robby and I didn't know at the time: Wachmann's mother Else and his sister Charlotte Philippine, two years older, were deported to the ghetto in Riga in 1942 and died there.

WATER ICE

Robby and I turn left at the University of Jena library and head for the Rose student beer cellar. Come on, he says, we can get in without tickets. The shoving at the entrance, the cast iron entrance door, then the steep steps, the stuffy but familiar atmosphere, the grubby vaulted ceiling. People standing everywhere, crowded together, holding their glasses. Planet earth is blue. And there's nothing I can do, booms out of the speakers. David Bowie. What do you think he does on the moon? Asks my brother. Who? – Major Tom. Looks for water ice. He's on a mission. – And after work, in the evening? – Does he need to smoke a joint and get laid. That's what he sings about. – Hey, is something the matter? He asks.

There are lots of beer cellars in Jena to go to in the evening. The Theaterkeller, the Schlosskeller, the Museumskeller. But none is as popular as the Rose. Only initiates know why and even they only discover the secret gradually. From the outside the uni club is just a bar like the rest, but inside it's the place where the Old World meets the New. Here am I sitting in a tin can. Far above the world, radios Major Tom from orbit, shortly before the contact is lost. On the tiny dance floor, bodies stuck to one another trying to lift off somehow. How quickly that can happen, I think. Perhaps we are all sitting in a capsule like the starman and slowly drifting away.

Robby and I fight our way through the masses with our beer glasses to halfway up the steps. That's where we like to stand. Clear view up and down. A bit like on a deer stand and as if from there we could see into the future. Below us the jerky red and blue dots on the dance floor. Like buoys at sea, rocking, bobbing, swaying and swallowed up by the crowd. We stand like lighthouse keepers on a cliff, well positioned. The more often we are in the Rose, the more we understand what's happening there. The signs, the processes. It is theatre, compulsive, simple, direct. The amount of information is enormous. Also the precision with which every single drama is orchestrated. Buoy A slowly approaches buoy D or buoys H and R strangely collide, and so on. It's about later in the night, about Western money, about business. The Rose is agitation, greed, lust, for many simply just the possibility of hanging out. It is the underground, the scene, El Dorado, prostitution, unification before the unification.

NOMADS

Robby's friend Sasha and his farewell party in April 1988. Tomorrow he won't be there anymore. Tomorrow morning he will be sitting in the train and in the evening with his relatives in Hamburg. He has been waiting two years for day X. In the background the punk band Feeling B booms: 'We want to be good all the time, because that's the only way people will like us.' A life of farewells, a constant thinning out. I'm stuck but feel like a nomad.

More and more frequently we sit in apartments in which people are saying goodbye or thinking of doing so. We go past windows where others were still living the day before. Now they're gone. Too much is gone and nothing takes its place. We drink.

There are maybe twenty people in the room. Among them are two friends of my brother who have also applied to leave. No one knows when they will be going. Sasha talks of Paris, of the Pont Neuf, of the Eiffel Tower. His aura is that of someone for whom the last evening has started. He goes from one person to the next, chatting, smoking, laughing, embracing. He wants to make it easy for himself and for us. His fear, the pressure, the secret service, his work ban – all of that is behind him. He looks exhausted, fragile and relieved, happy. He leaves something of himself behind and will take something of us with him. I look at him and think: this is how it starts.

These evenings, like caves with no way out. It's unbearable but no one can prise themselves away. It's a farewell for ever. Robby says to Sasha: you traitor. Else and Steffen laugh. A beer bottle rolls gently across the room. In the background Feeling B booms: 'Everyone lives their life completely alone and in the evening the stars fall.' My brother stands next to me. He would never have gone.

Historical instinct

NORTHERN LIGHTS. The train travelling to the Baltic via Poland and Brest on 23 August 1989 waited at the borders and went more and more slowly as it proceeded. Between Tallinn, Riga and Vilnius were two million people, a 600-kilometre chain, a human chain for freedom. Two million, holding hands, silent, crying, overjoyed, singing, with candles and flowers. The Baltic Way. The awakening. In the GDR everything was still closed. I travelled to Riga looking for grandfather, for a story that had not been told, that barely existed, and landed in the middle of a revolution.

Riga and the old silos, guilds and churches, the houses of the legendary merchant families – Reutern, Dannenstern, Mentzendorff. The ramshackle wooden houses on the banks of the Dauvaga, stinking of rancid fat. This is where the people assembled. They took out their tables, stacked raw fish, made bonfires and drank vodka like water. I recall the sea of candles on the river, the red animal meat, the endless batteries of schnapps glasses, the caraway black bread, the chicory coffee and the night-time rapture of freedom, which tasted of humility in the face of history. It was over. Finally. Again and again, attempts to describe this feeling fall short. There are events

that no one can influence. They take place and your only function is to be there merely to experience it. The people crouched
together, looked disbelievingly at the river, cried, smoked, sang
heartily and let the film roll.

The next day on my way to the national library on Tērbatas
iela. I was looking for the city's telephone directories from
1941 to 1945. They were thin, none had more than thirty or
forty pages, they smelled mouldy and had water stains.
Grandfather was listed from 1942 as government secretary at
Laudonstrasse 4. I crossed the Dauvaga to the state archives.
The city's housing registers were kept there. There were three
registers for Laudonstrasse 4 covering a whole century. But no
entry for Grunert. Finally, the files of the Reich Commissariat.
Worksheets, applications for allowances, travel expenses. Just
fragments. Most had been destroyed, or perhaps the copies
were somewhere in Germany. By chance I discovered an appli-
cation by grandfather in a pay file. But what did it say? Riga
was not the place to reconstruct the family history. Riga was
the place for a decision, a preliminary to my escape. I returned
again to East Berlin – to say farewell to Carla, my lifelong
friend, and to Robby. I had to see them both one more time.
There was no time left. I still remember that that is what I
thought – had been thinking for much too long.

In 1989, 343,854 East Germans left their homes, emigrated
or fled to find their feet in the new world – 343,854 endings
and new beginnings, projections and dreams, abandoning and
disappearing. I was one of them. I had not imagined earlier that
disappearing would be so complicated. People disappeared in
the fog, in a snow flurry, in a tunnel, dived into the sea or fell
into a deep valley. That happened. You read about that. But
this was a disappearance that required an idea, a plan and a
good portion of luck. Something that had to succeed. How was
I to arrange it? My head stuffed with all the old baggage, feeling
as if it were up against a wall. There was no plan. My thoughts
kept coming back on themselves like a broken record: you can

go, you can break loose, it's not so formidable, you don't have to hurry, it's possible. I was afraid.

I have no idea what I would have said if in summer 1989 someone had asked me about the year 2039. Not much probably, so as not to let anyone know about my escape. It could be that we are fainthearted when it comes to looking ahead to things that are important to us. The future of a successful revolution cannot be predicted. A miracle cannot be objectively controlled. And yet we can dream of the future, imagine horizons, breathe life into our illusions so ardently that they feel real. But I would have been way off the mark with my forecast for 1989. I simply couldn't conceive this happiest moment in history. My imagination didn't stretch that far. Later I sat with people on podiums who had organized the Pan-European Picnic on 19 August 1989, the first opening, the actual breakthrough. They spoke of secret service officers in the forests, troop movements, agreements, strategies, but above all of disillusionment. History, said one, is different from the image we have of it.

SEAMS. How will I speak, what will I look like, what will I think about, when I arrive in the new world? Who will I be? I didn't know. I just wanted to leave. To live my life. Nothing else. The night of escape from Kópháza. How do you manage to hold on to what really happened? And what happens to what remains, that has to remain, outside? I crawled through the darkness and thought of Robby. How he became smaller and smaller on the train platform in Dresden, until he disappeared behind a bend. I thought of Major Tom in his silver capsule who had also manoeuvred out of the darkness into the light. I had the clearest picture of how the starman in his silver spacesuit nosed his way centimetre by centimetre from his tin can into the blue immensity, then dangled despondently on his line to look out for the Earth, which was no longer to be seen. I was not the starman bobbing between the moon and Mars for

a last wave in the void. But I couldn't shake off the picture of
the lost man in the remote endlessness. It ran with me. He was
like my training partner. My route took me from Budapest to
Sopron, then Kópháza, and finally Vienna.

Vienna and the first days in the West. The German embassy
and the patient waiting. The city shimmered in my head like
mother-of-pearl. Bachmann of course, Musil and Bernhard.
For the first time to the Raimund, to Ungargasse 6, to the
Griensteidl and Bräunerhof coffeehouses. But the mythical places oppressed me more than they made me welcome.
Vienna was not the right place for this moment. I felt the
rutting, the pomp, the ambiguities even more intensely.

It was too compact, too chunky, too potent. I had nothing
to counter it with. My own baggage was heavy. There was no
curtain anymore, nowhere to hide. The outer and inner seams
were exposed, everything was in transition. It felt like an operation and as if I had laid myself open. I was dizzy. From Vienna
I went to a reception camp near Münster, and from there to
Frankfurt. I ended up in Darmstadt. It was coincidence, it was
Büchner. I don't know what it was.

The business with beginnings and how unique they are.
Welcome! Autumn 1989 and the special circumstances. The
accumulation, the symbolism, the euphoria. Some of it will
not dissolve. Some of it remains. Something that cannot be
dismissed. The feeling that everything was new and undeter-
mined. The feeling that suddenly anything was possible and
that there were endless new things to discover. The feeling of
control over your own life. There was no one anymore to stop
you, to interfere, to say no. We were left in peace. And that was
huge. It was the most important. The beginning, but a beginning without friends, without Robby, without a home, clothes,
books, money. I worked in a wine bar starting every day at
5 p.m. I lived in a servant's room with a washbasin, bed and
chair. I wore a pink dirndl, a white blouse with puffed sleeves
and was bald. I looked like what I was: ragged, weird, lost. And

that was how it was meant to be – pure, without a skin. No buffer, no padding.

Eight weeks later, Robby came to visit and with him some of the old familiarity returned. He was the first person to turn up in my interregnum in Hesse after the fall of the Berlin Wall. It was just before Christmas. We strolled through a city that we didn't understand. Blocks and lines, concrete and honeycomb buildings, corners with lots of wind, and the anonymity of the wide ring roads. It felt like a Mecca of the homeless. Scar tissue. Darmstadt has been the testing ground in September 1944 for the Dresden fire bombing, and its city centre had been completely destroyed. We went to see Beuys in the Landesmuseum, where he lived in his Block. Who in his lifetime built a residence in the upper storey and spread his heavy heart over seven rooms. The seven senses, the seven essential things, the Seven Swabians, seven as a lucky number. Beuys' *Trans-Siberian Railway*, *Scenes from the Deer Hunt*, *Chair with Fat*, *The Sled*. In the exhibition in East Berlin we could imagine. In Darmstadt everything was there to understand his pain.

My transitional me and Robby. We talked about what would have become of us if autumn 1989 hadn't happened. How many letters would have passed between us over the years, how we would have met occasionally in Prague or Budapest, how we would have done everything to maintain what we had together. Now there was no break, no pause. Alexander Kluge calls a successful revolution an 'alliance of all tracks through the sudden arrival of several messages in bottles in a safe haven'. Robby and I visited Frankfurt, Heidelberg, Mainz, Mannheim. The concerts, exhibitions, the first Asian meal, the short trips to France. In Strasbourg we drank champagne for the first time. The West was OK. It was not the enemy. My brother described the time as one of promise and returned home. I lived opposite Beuys' Block and started studying again. In Jena it had been literature, in Darmstadt philosophy.

MIRROR IMAGES. The pure times and the mental change of system. As if one had first run through a wide, empty plain. Starting a new life, in a shabby hotel, in clothes discarded by others and given to me, with everything I left behind and what could happily stay there. In retrospect, the mental images of the beginning are bathed in a warm light. But nothing was just left as it was. There was also no clean slate. The slate was not blank. 'The decisive principle of action of "socialism as it really existed" was violence,' wrote the psychoanalyst Hans-Joachim Maaz in the psychogram *Gefühlsstau* published in 1991. The dictatorship of the walls, the violence and the emptiness. As I sat in autumn 1989 in the West somewhere in a seminar room or café I could hear something in me still rattling. A dull, thunderous sound, like a mountain subsiding. Shields, jagged peaks, endless boulders. Internalized feelings are separate planets with their own laws.

Something was over but it wouldn't lie still. Everyone could feel how the political tectonic plates were beginning to shift. But what happened during that slippage to perpetrators and victims, to actors and followers, to crypt and phantom, to memory and experience? I imagine billions of experiences wandering around our bodies, moving from cell to cell, continuously evoking realities, history and narratives; I imagine them rejoicing, stumbling, laughing or delirious in a bid to deal with pain and hurt. We can leave those experiences to stew inside us, shrug them off, reject them, separate them; we can transpose them to the reality of dreams or the imagination or try to reconcile them with real life. We were in this holding phase, in the interim of history, and were full to the brim with the internalized state, with pressure, fear, violence, silence. We had the joy of redemption, but what were we to do with our experiences? How to come to terms with them? How to understand them? The tripwires of history. We weren't emerging from a war. The buildings were still standing, however dilapidated. We were emerging from the regime of an internal war.

That too had been swept away by the revolution. But what did that mean? And did it offer us any certainty?

The celebrated Zero Hour, which hadn't existed after 1945, and the new period of rewriting after 1989. National Socialism as a disaster for Germany, and autumn 1989 as the great piece of good fortune. The starting-up periods after the two German dictatorships are not analogous and yet they were mirror images. I know I will fail, that it's impossible to describe, but I am interested in the character of our experience, our mental images. 'The magic, the demonic, if you like,' wrote Nobel Prize winner Imre Kertész, 'is that the story of totalitarianism demands our entire existence but, after we have given ourselves completely to it, leaves us in the lurch, simply because it continues differently, with a fundamentally different logic.'

TRIPWIRES. Giving completely, left in the lurch, the fundamentally different logic. Something we couldn't see at the time because it was too powerful. We couldn't accept it, not yet. I see a ship on its way to the North Pole, on an endless journey to the pack ice. I see containers passing me by, on ships, every day putting out aimlessly to sea, with a cargo that no one wants anymore, that has to be got rid of. Where shall we put all this East stuff? The baggage with everything that loaded us down, the resignation, the incomprehension, the waving aside, the unfulfilled expectations, the abandoned dreams, the hushed-up stories, the forsaken yearnings – the last news from an unloved land. The year of revolution and what was forcefully flushed away and covered over, what remained unacknowledged and what was to endure. Perhaps this turbulent time can be described at least from the internal images?

Like when I flew from Frankfurt for the first time to Berlin to see friends again. That was January 1990. How we went to bars in Berlin-Mitte. Grubby, techno, abandoned. A city without rules or control. Every night a new reality. Demolition, beginning, the unhoped-for. Something that exploded with such vehemence and was already buried again. Drifting, we sifted through experiences, enjoyed being aimless, were eager to relax. As if time had no plans.

Like when I took my driving test in Darmstadt and set off on my first trip to Jena. Endless roadworks on the autobahn between Erfurt and Weimar. Mountains of debris, as if we were in no-man's land. And between, streams of brand-new Western cars, practically all with Erfurt, Weimar and Jena number plates. A traffic jam on that day that would not clear, with people behaving as if it were the most natural thing in the world – leaving their cars, chatting with one another, exchanging technical banter, appearing not to feel particularly troubled. I looked at tired, pale faces. I saw in them scarred landscapes. As if the new cars the people were leaning against only underlined the bitterness of their lives.

There were lots of jigsaw pieces in me containing bits of the new beginning. Breaking up, breaking in, breaking out. Of all this, how much belongs to me? When will I know that the beginning is over? And what will happen to the submerged historical legacy? Autumn 1989 and what it covered up. The revolution and its delusional moment. It was not just about the billions of SED assets that had been sequestered overseas, the memory of the East shredded and thus cut in half by the secret service in autumn 1989, the quiet transformation of old structures into the new system. It was also about the fundamentally different logic in us, through which the regime continued to exist. What is really over, what do we suppress, what do we push away? What did we take with us into this new era, and what did we really let go of? What are our blind spots?

Every generation clings to its identity. There are reference systems, stereotypes, political coordinates or, as the sociologist Karl Mannheim wrote in the 1920s, 'lifestyles, habits and a specific generational discourse'. The post-war generation, the war children who created the GDR and allowed the regime to continue. The grandchildren, the only generation that specifically

sought to end the GDR. They were not interested in reform –
they actually excluded it as an option. A generation that spoke
out clearly and put into practice what they said: end, over,
finished. If this generation had a destiny, then it was to see
how far it would succeed in transforming the violence it had
been exposed to. Or how much this experience would become
the story of its hate. 'The meaning of revolutions is to be found
in their negation *and* in the new start *and* in the search for
something new,' writes the historian Ilko-Sascha Kowalczuk.

MAGNETIC FIELDS

Robby and I on a trip from Darmstadt to Marseille. The
dented, silver-grey Fiat. A thousand kilometres of motorway,
via Freiburg, Valence, Avignon, then Marseille. The first time
in the south, the first café beyond the border. Our smashed
windows, Robby's stolen camera, our visit to the gendarmerie.
Two policemen behind a desk, rocking backwards and forwards on their chairs and smirking. Non, non, non. Shrug of
the shoulders. If you don't speak French, you don't exist. We
drive to a garage and continue with new glass.

Marseille and the seagulls with their incessant monologue.
The white spray of another, warmer life that seems somehow
to seal itself off. The port, the rubbish, like looking into the
world's sewer. The black men that the sea has thrown up and
who lie in the dirt as if it were a well-heated day room. Robby
and I want to go swimming, so we drive on to Bandol. The
narrow corridors in the small hotel by the beach. The lime
green wallpaper, in which hundreds of little fish swim up and
down.

The nights are light. We sit by the sea and drink red wine.
Not a single star yet in the sky. My brother whispers softly:
Look! And points to the waves. There's something there. Two
bodies coming out of the water. Two turtles leaving the sea and

scurrying blindly across the sand. Their paddles leave precise rectangular prints. They build nests, burrow busily, lay their eggs, quickly wipe away the traces and waddle over the sand back into the water. Busy, silent, the shells shimmering in the light. A play as if under a charm, performed only to ward off the dangers. To survive. The pair don't notice us. They just want to disappear, become invisible, slip softly into the sea. The water is fragrant. The stillness falls over us. There are turtles here? I ask Robby in surprise. They can go anywhere, he says. They are guided by the Earth's magnetic field.

Exhalations

ROUND ONE. Magnetic fields and the double-bind of dis-
solution where everything is in motion. Do we also move? The
principle of dissociation and the possibility of not managing
to do so. The family as a social capsule and 'psychic agency
of society', as the psychologist Erich Fromm put it. And what
happens when the inner and outer capsules break open at the
same time?

Hoyerswerda, 1991. The five days in September and the
first pogrom. It has been well documented. 'What will happen
when the time bomb explodes?' asked the *Hoyerswerder
Wochenblatt* in 1990, the year of unification. The question
referred to the high unemployment, the insecurity following
the fall of the Berlin Wall, the open racism in the city. Barely
a year later, incendiary bombs, bottles and stones were being
thrown at a contract workers' hostel in Schweitzer-Strasse.
Windows were broken. Army songs were sung, 'Germany for
Germans – foreigners go home!' chanted the attackers. The
crowd jeered and clapped. For a fraction of a second, the live
reports on television channels all over the world showed the
faces of the hostel residents. Young men from Mozambique,
Angola, Ghana, Cuba. Sheer panic in their eyes. Down on the

streets hundreds of neo-Nazis and skinheads had ganged up
in order to storm the building. Their determined stances, the
flames themselves, an emergency situation if ever there was
one. The police stood by and watched. The situation looked like
it could well escalate – and did so, as the marchers moved on
to a nearby hostel for asylum seekers. Persecution, hounding,
fights, injuries. Until the prey were evacuated from the city after
a few days to jeers and applause. It was a victory of the street, an
expulsion, capitulation. Hoyerswerda became a symbol. That's
where it began, people were to say later. 'Ausländerfrei' – free
of foreigners – the un-word of the year 1991.

Rostock-Lichtenhagen in summer 1992. The Sunflower
House, the central refugee reception centre in Mecklenburg-
Western Pomerania. The refugees, above all from Romania,
camped out for weeks in front of the new prefabricated building. The centre completely overcrowded. Outside no food, no
water, no toilets. The conditions were becoming chaotic. The
second pogrom was announced in advance and was dubbed
a 'people's festival', a 'spontaneous public insurrection', 'a
great fire'. The images were similar to those in Hoyerswerda:
mostly young men, Wall children, war grandchildren. In cam-
ouflage trousers and t-shirts with the inscription 'Sieg Heil!'
They were mobilized, rampaged through the 'other scene of
action', as Freud named the lost race for a point of reference,
a limit, a prohibition. 'Humanity is a universe full of children
through which the category of the mythical father runs,' wrote
the French legal historian Pierre Legendre.

The site of the violence, the drama on television and the
public in uproar. The inside and the outside, the German and
the alien, good and evil, the determination to destroy and the
extrovert coma. The first round of the asylum seeker complex
in the new Germany. The images revealed something that
smacked of a witch hunt, of archaic rituals, of emptiness and
extreme brutality. They showed how a society could simply
fall apart, split into hunters and hunted. The scent had been

picked up. Such things were now possible. A hand-to-hand combat, an extreme reaction in a vacuum that instantly called forth imitators. The pogrom climate spread to West Germany. Saarlouis, Mölln, Solingen. Racist attacks, now also with fatalities. Politicians spoke of a state of emergency. In May 1993 a more restrictive asylum policy was adopted. It was one of the last laws by the government in Bonn.

HOPEFUL PRONOUNCEMENTS. The rapid and plausible story of unification – the new Germany wanted it, perhaps even needed it. The division was healed, the two sides were now one. So where was the problem? I read the old hopeful pronouncements by Helmut Kohl, by Hans-Dietrich Genscher. It is the tone rather than the content that haunts me. As if a radio was only playing hits from the 1950s. The fake cosiness, the containment, the patina of a post-war decade prepared to ignore anything that might not fit the narrative. That's quite something, I think later: how many disparate elements the opaque tone was able to blank out from the very outset. Kohl, born in 1930, Genscher, born in 1927, two political architects of West Germany with the historical certainty of having done everything right. I thought of father and how he might have felt on 9 November 1989. What did he make of the cheering crowds in Berlin? What went through his mind? What did he say? Did he feel bad?

The hoped-for information in the documents about myself. In 1992 I applied from Darmstadt to see my Stasi file. I was thirty-two years old. I thought I should know what had gone on. The GDR had been history for three years. A world set to last for ever was gone. I could see the prospect of standing on solid ground. My file was one of the possible paths. I remember the strange uneasy feeling I had as I set off in the silver-grey Fiat on the autobahn to Gera. That's where the file was. What would happen if I were to read something I didn't want to know about? Was I betrayed by love? Was I controlled by the state?

That makes it sound as if my file is something special. It isn't. It contains operative personal checks between 1984 and 1986 recorded in two volumes that I was finally able to see in 1994.

The building where the file was stored: it could not have had more of a flavour of the East. The room where I was able to read them: the plastic tables, the overgrown rubber plant, the acrid smell of cleanser. The man who handed me the file asked: do you need any explanations? I shook my head. Archives are time vaults. Sometimes they let you return from the new world to the old. They know how to make the transition. But what happened in Gera? A new life, above all an independent one – that's why I'd fled to the West in summer 1989. The interregnum years, my transition. Where did I belong? I would like to be able to describe it from the beginning: how I entered a room and the dossier was there, how I leafed through every page, how I read and how nothing was the same afterwards. The words in the file were old words from an old world. But they determined everything that was to come. There was no return after the room with the rubber plant.

GUARD OF HONOUR. I want to remember, to look back. Where was Robby during this interim period? When I was in Gera reading my file, he was clambering around old steamships from the Weisse Flotte, visiting abandoned cloth mills and a disused tram terminus. His photos had a single theme: disappearance. He called them timeless pictures. 'I had to enter illegally,' he wrote in his workbook, 'because these sites were cordoned off. No one will focus the camera again and use it as I did. But ultimately these photos were just records, photographic realism in the narrow sense. I was always too late for the reality.' My brother who felt too late for the reality and therefore put himself in his photos. 'I crawl out into the world as if from a cave. I jump, I'm in transition, there and not there.'

Robby wanted to see what happened if he put himself in his pictures. As if he wanted to feel at home in them, to find a place that was his own visual echo. I look at his pictures. Once again the confusion, the blurring. The clock on them always says quarter past twelve, the light is always dazzling, his face always out of focus. My brother constructed a space in which he sought his place in an abandoned world. But what was he doing there? What was I doing at that time? What were the others from our generation doing?

Everyone was setting off, everyone was searching. For the children of the divided Germany, everything was possible, it was said. It was a time of great schemes, dreams, new geography. We stood at the airports of the world and gazed at the sky. Why only two lives? There could just as easily be a third. The Wall generation were said to be the lucky ones. And it was true. For them, the 1989 revolution came at the best time in their lives. After the upheaval they studied or trained again according to Western standards. It was not difficult for them to integrate into the new Germany. At least, that's what the sociologists said. But was that really true? When I think about us, what comes to mind most vividly is Heiner Müller's poem 'Traumwald', from 1994. It describes a man running through a winter forest, passing animals on his way. They form a guard of honour, frozen in the frost and arranged alphabetically. A landscape of war, dream and theatre. A child in armour with a lance comes up to him. The child will kill the man. 'And in the blink of an eye between thrust and penetration,' it says, 'my face looked at me: the child was me.' Very dramatic, it's true, but I have never found anything more valid, nothing that refers so directly and unambiguously to our generation. The war, the dream, the armour, the armoured child in us. I want to try to keep this child in mind.

Because what was happening in the second half of our lives? What were we doing with the good fortune that we had been privileged to be handed by history? When I wake up, I can sometimes taste a quite specific time. The 1990s. It tastes uncooked, unsettled, unclear, immoderate. From May 1992 the inquiry commission 'Processing and consequences of the SED dictatorship'. Seventy-six hearings, forty plenary sessions, six years of dispute: so, what was it exactly, the GDR? At its heart an East-West debate, sometimes fierce, sometimes flippant, sometimes condescending, but decided from the outset. The philosopher Jürgen Habermas, who set the tone, spoke of a 'dispute about the punctuation of history'. The GDR as a foot-note in the history of the world, as a comma, a semicolon. It didn't even merit a question mark in the eyes of the Western elites. The curtain to the East remained closed. The dynamics of guilt and resentment dominated. In 1995 the second com-mission. Three years later its final report: thirty-one volumes, 36,000 pages. The country behind the curtain was thus taken care of. And at a time when major groups of victims in it didn't even realize that they had been victims.

The asynchronism of the experiences, hopes, breaks, over-load, silence. I drove to Dresden, to Saxon Switzerland, up the Hockstein, back to my parents for the first time since my flight. It was September 1995. I entered a house that I didn't know, one where I'd practically never been. The view from the bench in front of the kitchen window in the direction of the Bastei was magnificent. On the kitchen table was the last issue of *Die Rote Fahne*.[1] I was taken aback. At supper, my mother, look-ing at me, said that everything was good again. What do you mean? I asked. Robby interrupted and said that he was going to demolish the barn the next day, that he had met Sasha, who was back in Dresden, and that he would finish his studies in eighteen months.

MOTHER'S BAGGAGE. Brother and sister, nearness and loss. In retrospect it's this evening with my parents that decided that the alienation also belongs in this book. We never know

---

[1] The official newspaper of the Communist Party of Germany during the time of the German Democratic Republic.

exactly where it begins, look back helplessly later on, search inside, listen again to the tone of the sentences, and still can't find the point where the strangeness first appeared. How were we seated together? Father had lived at least eight other lives. And each of them had been without inhibitions. Mother knew about and shared responsibility for everything. Not a word spoken about it. Nothing. The only indication the *Rote Fahne* that someone had pushed onto the corner bench. If I just begin to think about the way the unspoken was also present. Father's hands, paddling above, next to and under the table. Mother's eyes, glancing furtively at the garden or looking for Robby. He was what gave her stability. In retrospect the words at the family table. Could there have been something there after all in what was left unspoken? The evening had no message, no focus, no echo. Masked, strange. We sat there as if we didn't know each other. Moment after moment. What was left was a diffuse feeling. The most important was cut out, the most necessary left unsaid.

To a certain extent, this way of being absent also applied to East German society after 1989. There is certainly enough to say about the self-imposed regime of silence, the silence of the political powers – about the Muscovites and their Stalin trauma, the red Buchenwald inmates, the killing fields of two world wars, victims and perpetrators. But ultimately all of the silence finds its home in a single, specific life and becomes experience. Then the words are withheld for self-protection, made to appear harmless, unspoken so as to make sure that nothing is felt.

What might have changed after 1989? How? Why? Were there not even more reasons for keeping quiet after this second upheaval? The psychology of the dual dictatorship with its explosive turbulence, all the unexplained, suppressed, passed on from generation to generation. I think of mother, who was more resolute in her refusal to speak than anyone I have ever met. She would pause, turn away, hesitate, look subdued, feign surprise, pull a face, fail to react or simply refuse to reply. Her silence had something breathless about it. A silence that concealed, dissimulated, said nothing, covered up, ignored, refused to respond, skirted the issue. It was no doubt the system she needed, the ultimate control and triumph.

The small, silent woman with the tired eyes, who had struggled all her life with the archaic guilt, starting as a six-year-old responsible for the accidental death of her three-year-old brother. October 1941, when the inner clock stopped suddenly at the hidden bend in front of her childhood home. The girlish longing for her own doll that was never to be fulfilled. Not to have to bear the longing, the guilt – which wasn't real – on her own. Sometimes, when in my imagination I sit next to mother to ask her questions, I run with her down the street away from this unhappy bend, past the fields and apple trees, past the church, to her school, and I ask myself how a child can continue living with such a shock. I don't know. I just see this girl with the scared eyes taking a taxi with her mother and siblings from Tilsit to Riga. An abandoned girl, who took a journey into the great abandon that never abandoned her again. The accident, Riga, the flight through the Baltic in summer 1944, the bombing of Dresden a good six months later. At the end of this ordeal she was just ten years old.

Fear, absence, silence, guilt feelings. It is the glue that holds together the inner spaces of post-war families in East and West. War children with no dolls or balls, but still having to find room somewhere for their transferred guilt. Not every child was as exposed as mother, but the question of guilt was the internal bond, the common theme. When I sit in my imagination next to mother to ask her questions, even when I know that she will never answer me, I start with the bend where the accident took place and her heart standing still. I know it can't be right. But what should I do? How can this mother start explaining, when she has been silent of her own volition for fifty years? The moment when my uncle died in 1941 as a three-year-old.

He became her cover story, the safe image behind which are hidden other images that can't be talked about. But perhaps mother conjured up this primal scene again and again during her life and repeated it so as to find another solution to her first fright, to make it go away and to expunge it.

It sounds plausible from the outside. Here the cause, there the effect, two or three sentences, and everything takes on a new meaning. But mother's baggage is more complicated. More inaccessible, more withdrawn, more hidden, more indistinct. As if having to penetrate an endlessly indifferent fog. It takes something from what is there and won't go away, but I have to get through it. This time it's not any imagined questions. Mother and I are really sitting opposite one another. I ask her my questions. Always the same: what role did the man without inhibitions play in your life? Or, why did you allow all that to happen to us? Or, what did grandfather really do in Riga? Whether real or imagined questions, it's all very well to ask, but there won't be any answers. Just the fog that seems to me like a tunnel. One that has no beginning because there isn't one. What is it like to hide your entire life?

The law of caution, not attracting attention at any cost, appearing not to have any demands. The law of boundless pupation. Mother gave birth to five children, raised four of them and worked full-time throughout. When I sit next to her and look at her from the side, I think immediately of Emerenc, the thin maid in István Szabó's film *The Door*. I see Helen Mirren in Budapest in the 1960s. Shovelling snow, putting food on trays, slaving away wordlessly before disappearing in the evening behind her door, where she has secretly stowed her story away. She is disturbingly strange with her limitless mastery, self-control, self-sacrifice. I follow Helen Mirren, cocooned in her world of silence, and think all the time that I'm seeing something different: a very silent woman who actually wants to scream. She doesn't do it once. Nor does mother. Never.

The young post-war mothers in toxic proximity to the

history they carried inside themselves forever. Strong and
hungry for life, weak and shattered, unfathomable and destructive, all at the same time. An ambivalence that led them to
build a wall of denial and authority that they imposed on their
children. Wiliness, anxiety, constant vigilance. These children
interpreted and listened to the mother figures drifting away,
took in their regard and waited for affection. It came, without
question, but never directly. It was affection of a more difficult, more unfathomable kind involving repression at others'
expense, lies to secure their own position, a complicated system
of punishment and reward, support that was meant to shame
the absentee, maternal hatred delegated to the father.

This is written here because the picture of the beaming
emancipated East German woman became the reference after
1989. The East German woman as guiding light, as blueprint
for the new gender sound after the unification of Germany. It
is the image of the tough worker, hard pressed from all sides,
whose public reputation was created by making the impossible
possible: the happy reconciliation of work and family. The East
German success model of the 'progressive woman' was that of
a mother with at least two children, working full-time, socially
active, steadfastly managing household and children, needless
to say with an unclouded lust for life. This is the multi-tasker,
the universal mother, who in the new Germany needs only to
transform herself from an East German to a West German
woman.

This image of the East German woman is fragile and changing, depending on the perspective, generation and experience
and whether it is viewed from the inside or the outside. Can a
common denominator be found nevertheless for this myth? Or,
what was the question of authority really about? Who ruled the
state? Where was the East German woman in the institutions,
the economy, the universities, at the controls in the country?
What shaped her everyday family life? Where were the policies
made, not for the mythical wife but for the real women? In

reality, no state was more patriarchal than East Germany. A traditional structure, in which women were defined by men, and not only symbolically. In reality as well they were stuck in the background, slaving away, keeping everything under control, making the decisions, carrying out the tasks and often enough making sure they were done.

Our strong mothers and their miserable lack of responsibility, who did not stop their husbands' violence but often enough let it happen, looked away, kept quiet, lived with it or even participated themselves. Shame and betrayal, lies and blame, self-controlled and completely shut off, biographies and family memories, in a personal silence politicized through fifty-six years of dictatorship and still possessed by the East after 1989. How to get beyond it?

MASCULINITY. I think of Markus, a school friend, who told me that when he was playing, his mother used to put a rope round his neck because that was the only way for her to control his wild nature. I think of the stories told to me by my friend Hans, whose mother placed him between her and his father in bed at night. To this day, he relives the memory of the excesses. I think of Simone, a fellow student, whose mother allowed her to be sadistically tortured by her father in order to shield their son. This was just one version of the thick fog: the mother dissolving into the aggressive shadow of the father while at the same devising a system of control over her own children.

Of course there were the others: the caring mothers, who built up an intimate alliance with their children, the tight-knit communities formed out of the need for mothers to seek refuge from the fathers' violence; the helpless, incapable mothers, who lived on with their children in the face of the men silenced by war; or the courageous ones, who took their children to escape finally from the cycle of violence. It was women who were the first to storm the Stasi headquarters in Leipzig and Erfurt in 1989 and grab hold of the sceptre of revolution.

And yet, in the cool clear light of day, despite the different living constructs available to them, the proud East German women were unable to overturn the male authority. However modern women's politics in East Germany looked to the outside world, however visible women became, particularly from the 1970s onwards, East Germany remained stubbornly a system based on a strong father image and hence on a male dictator. At the core of the system, the polarized Nazi ideals of masculinity and femininity were retained and, if anything, supplemented by a Soviet component: the life-giving, child-bearing women under the Nazis met the image of the working mother as a 'builder of communism'. In an ambivalent process, the image of women was masculinized and exploited. On the other hand, the expanded role granted to them also produced a rare self-image that later enabled careers like that of Angela Merkel.

DREAM MACHINE

Robby and I are lounging on the green leather sofa in my Kreuzberg apartment. It is the mid-1990s and we are talking about our dreams.

He: At night frogs keep coming to my bed and jumping on my chest.

Me: I was standing at a bar and a toothless man mumbled a toast to me: You know there is a truth behind every imagined story.

He: In my dreams the women always have bad breath.

Me: I am sitting on the toilet in a large, empty apartment in an old building in Berlin. That's all.

He: I would love to have erotic dreams.

Me: I see a thin, ragged girl who can't stop running and I think that's not a dream.

He: I long for fur and imagine a whole animal kingdom that doesn't exist in reality.

Me: At the end of the dream was mother, who said: If you can't find your way back alone you can't go out.

He: I dream that I am reading something that bores me to death and I fall asleep in the dream.

Me: We are crossing the Atlantic on an old ocean liner. In the middle of the ocean, it breaks into two. You carry on sailing on one half and me on the other.

World of taboos

CHANGES. The armour of the war grandchildren. I had promised to keep it in view. It's about Robby, mother and the revolution. In 1989, this small, quiet woman lived with a defeated man. It was her defeat as well, but as was the case after 1945, there was once again the excuse. To be a woman in itself softened the question of complicity. The essay by Katharina Rothe and Oliver Decker, 'Gefühlserbschaften des Nationalsozialismus und Geschlecht' [The emotional legacy of National Socialism and gender] analyses the degree to which women downplayed and trivialized National Socialism. But who knows really what women and men do with what under normal circumstances would be called guilt? How did mother feel about the implosion of the much-vaunted GDR project? In 1989 she was fifty-four years old. When I saw her again she was sixty. Had anything changed for her at all?

How much she was able to say by being silent. How much she was able to decide by doing nothing. My parents had been living for ten years in their house on the Hockstein that father's Stasi commanding officer had arranged for them. It was a hiding place, just as the grandparents had hidden after 1945. The *Rote Fahne* provided the orientation, the old networks reported back, it was about consolidation. Who wants to have lost? I notice that I seem to be quite on my own with this topic. How should I talk about it, how can I imagine it? I look for books, material that describes this state from the inside. A surprising amount has been written. Practically half of the old Politburo people sat down after 1989 and wrote their memoirs, some of them more than once. The hole in the swansong narrative had to be filled. If everyone talked about it quickly enough, it wouldn't be so bad. It was about the legacy and controlling how it was seen, the defining authority and the new beginning. The guilt question? That could be crossed off fairly easily.

One reason was because the legal processing inevitably left gaps. It had already become clear after the first dictatorship that courtrooms were not the right place for this reprocessing. A thousand people executed, hundreds killed while attempting to escape, 700 injured by mines and spring guns, 12,000 carted off to Soviet labour camps, more than 250,000 political prisoners, over 50 murder and over 600 kidnapping plots – all of this was part of the illegal activities by the GDR. But they had no force, they made no impression. The perpetrator elite did not even have to really pause. Of 100,000 investigations after 1989, only 1 per cent led to prosecution. Forty people were imprisoned without probation. Forty people for forty years of dictatorship? It's not the numbers but the measure. How was this whitewashing possible? The leniency of the rule of law, which immediately emboldened the perpetrators and organized their silence. Why admit anything when there is no demand for satisfaction? 'In political terms we should not ask what will become of the individual who tells the truth but what will become of the world in which the truth is concealed or not told. It will become a world of taboos,' wrote Hannah Arendt in 1963 in her *Denktagebücher*.

The world of taboos that in the fog generated by the perpetrators was made to disappear without problem. The fog: the new 'field of operations', the unified Germany, in which the old East German clientele was well buffered thanks to the billions stolen and was thus able to completely reorganize. The networks functioned effectively, their members obtained comfortable pensions 'for their life's work', entered parliament, occupied high positions in the administration, launched careers in culture, the media and sport, inaugurated campaigns in the East German province against journalists critical of the GDR, attacked victims at events, initiated vicious readers' letter campaigns, created a new Young Guard, and once again set up shop in Dubai and Shanghai to develop brand-new networks.

The Gesellschaft zur rechtlichen und humanitären Unterstützung [Society for Legal and Humanitarian Support] was founded in 1993 as a lobby organization for the former GDR nomenklatura. It continues to publish books, operate websites, meet in almost 200 local groups, organize nationwide events, support the perpetrators financially or in finding lawyers, and employ tried-and-tested 'decomposition' ['*Zersetzung*'] strategies to make life difficult again for the victims. The long-term agenda behind this historical looping was clear: the gradual disappearance from public attention of historical facts and perpetrator biographies, contamination of society with a world of taboos, and strategic reorientation in a global media world.

I can't say how much father continued to be active in the new 'field of operations'. It is clear that the secret service was still part of him. I say that today because I am able to observe him in retrospect from the other side of his world, as if through a looking glass. It sounds a bit complicated. And it was. I learned to read the subtexts.

STILL THE SAME. In 1996 I left Darmstadt and went to Berlin. A room with a coal-fired stove in a back courtyard in Kreuzberg. I visited the federal archive in Finckensteinallee and the Stasi document authority in Berlin-Mitte. It was my way of confronting the fog and the world of taboos. I didn't know how else to go about it.

The armour of the war grandchildren. I drove through Dresden with Robby in my old Fiat. We cruised through Brandenburg to look at village churches. We sat in the car and trusted in the landscape that passed us by, the people at the traffic lights behind their steering wheels, the houses, the bridges, the world. We trusted in the privacy of the situation and the armour around us. It had sorted out everything for us. I read Robby's letters from this time lying in front of me, all written on ochre yellow paper. He writes: 'You're still the same sister you were for me when I visited you in Jena, in Darmstadt, right at the beginning. I would still travel to visit you with the same feeling. But we are very far apart. And there is also the time that separates us.'

His still-the-same and the separation through space and time. As if we no longer surfaced in the here and now. It's true, we didn't see each other very often, three or four times a year. But isn't life like that? Robby stayed where he was, in Dresden, in the family. He had finished his studies and was an art teacher. I sat in the archive, in Berlin, and started to write. My first book was published in 1996. I want to find words because otherwise I can't hear Robby's voice. And without words he isn't here. Without words I feel lost and can't go forward. This way I might find the connection to him. I remember the afternoon in the palliative care unit, when I saw him again after five years. You have to keep the balls in the air, he said, otherwise you'll be trapped. I can see his right hand, the thumb and index finger opening and closing, as if the hand was breathing. As if it were a trap opening and closing. My brother could just as well have drawn circles in the air, or let his hand lie on the blanket, or gently stroked his head. Instead, he thought of balls and how he became a juggler. I try to recall Robby's face.

Trap, confusion, balls, blurring. 'I have often thought about what you said to me last time you visited me in Dresden – that we would be able to speak less and less,' I read in a letter written in January 1998. I can see it clearly, the writers' conference a few weeks earlier in Jena chaired by the author Jürgen Fuchs. How he started by talking about Manès Sperber, then the implosion of history in people's souls, the silence of the East, the incredibly long time working in the shadows. He spoke about a 'fight for memory' as a fight for facts. I had met Jürgen Fuchs several times since 1994, mostly in one of the Berlin file repositories. We talked as if we had always done so. That's how he was. 'What touches me about Sperber,' he said in Jena, 'is his attempt to respond artistically, intellectually and existentially to the depths, dangers and inner strife of the individual and time. Our time as well, that we're in the thick of.'

The still-the-same, the in-the-thick-of-it, the separation in space and time. Jürgen Fuchs in a seminar room at the University of Jena. He appeared hurt, spoke insistently, gesticulating, hurriedly, shivering. Everything about him was hectic. He was already seriously ill. Beads of sweat glistened on his forehead. The chemicals, he said, and casually wiped his brow. I told him about the unpublished texts from East Germany and that I had started to look for them. I told him about Edeltraud Eckert, the poet, who died in 1955 at the age of twenty-five in an East German prison. Do you know her? I asked. No, but there must be stuff written about her, it must be there, he insisted. As recollection, as evidence, as a draft. He named names, contacts, had ideas. When I thought about him later, I thought of protocols and operations, grammar and latency, bone marrow and wounds healing. I thought of Büchner. 'Every fear that we imagine puts us at a disadvantage,' wrote Herta Müller.

I had wanted to tell Robby about this encounter, about a scene that remained undiscussed, open like those years, about the few telephone conversations and visits to Jürgen Fuchs at Tempelhof airport, about his uncomplaining despair at the inescapable diagnosis that faced him. He died in May 1999. The café in Dresden-Neustadt where I wanted to tell my brother about the funeral at the Heidefriedhof in Berlin, about Wolf

Biermann with the guitar, about Ralph Giordano with the silk scarf, about the hundreds who came across the field to take their leave of him.

I know my brother's repertoire for avoiding entering into conversation: stroking his lips contemplatively with his thumb, touching first the right then the left ear, raising his eyebrows, smiling his distant smile, his half-trusting, half-suspicious gaze. I didn't have the impression that he wasn't interested in what I was saying, but he couldn't say anything. Or didn't want to. Or didn't want to because he couldn't. Or both. It was like talking to a wall. Nothing came back. I wasn't reaching him. The armour of the war grandchildren that had got locked in underneath the armour of the war children. The phantom and the crypt. I want to say that there is no single causality, no right or wrong. There are never direct connections but only indirect ones. The fog, the world of taboos. What we do and what we don't do.

JENA AND THE NSU. Jürgen Fuchs in November 1997 in a seminar room at his old university, the gurgling radiators, his words, going headlong forwards, as if they were on the run and had to get out. His struggle with the tamed revolution and the crack in history, which he fell into. Sometimes I'm sitting around, in a café, don't know what to do and suddenly feel the full weight of time. Then there's the seminar room in Jena full of authors and civil rights activists, practically all born in the 1950s: Lutz Rathenow, Gabriele Stötzer, Eve and Frank Rub, Doris Liebermann, who knew each other from the time in opposition. They had 'kicked out', as Jürgen Fuchs would have said, and overthrown the regime. It was finished but not gone. The days in Jena were about how it was not possible for it to be gone. I recall words such as revenants, ghosts, outcasts. Jürgen Fuchs spoke of defects and shadows. He was not only a writer but also a psychologist. He was making a point. Something that was finished but not gone.

The weight of time on me as I walk around Jena, past the seminar room to the Löbdergraben, where the number 2 tram stops on its way to Winzerla. The urban panorama: the factory chimneys, the chalk hills, the precast concrete housing estates up there next to the autobahn. All of it constantly visible. On the left, in Altlobeda, my old student apartment. A world close enough to see and feel: Jena and the ancient university with its 20,000 students. The city of Hegel, Schiller, the early Romantics, Ricarda Huch and the Bauhaus architects. During the GDR period, a city of air pollution and crisis. Empty fruit and vegetable shops, queues at the butcher's, roads in disrepair, shortage of doctors, cleaned-out department stores, scarce housing, crowded buses all the time. A city bursting constantly at the seams and imploding on itself. A question of centrifugal forces, or a special kind of boiler pressure perhaps.

I lived in Jena for twelve years. It's surprising how much events mean or how we speak through them. The November meeting, the overheated seminar room and a coincidence that would only be discovered years later. Some things need time. The thing with the defects, for example. What Jürgen Fuchs was attempting so insistently to name was long taking place just a few kilometres away. Except that we didn't know. A whole society didn't know. Jena and November 1997, where Uwe Mundlos and Uwe Böhnhardt, the two men from the future National Socialist Underground (NSU) terrorist cell, had been playing around with TNT at garage number 5 in the Kläranlage complex. The Thuringia intelligence services were already on the scent of these two neo-Nazis. Weeks later, on 26 January 1998, on a cold Monday, a raid was to be carried out. The story is well known: the garage, the police, the explosives, and how the killer trio were able to calmly disappear underground. They lived in hiding under false names for as long as Angela Merkel had ruled the united Federal Republic in 2018. Thirteen years.

The 26th of January 1998, the day it was said that the NSU could have been prevented. Nothing was prevented. The day was a disaster and a symbol. On that day the terrorist trio were allowed to disappear underground unhindered and later to come out of hiding and carry out ten murders, forty-three attempted murders, at least three bomb attacks and fifteen robberies. Following on from this 26th of January 1998, as Harald Range, Attorney General at the Federal Court of Justice, summed up in one short sentence: 'The NSU murders are our 9/11.' The beginnings, the perpetrators, the victims, the terror. So much has been written. But how can something that consists of just three people be called an 'underground'? Where is the context, the system of accomplices and suppliers, the networks?

Jena and the new actors: the third East German generation, the unification children, Hitler's great-grandchildren and their story of hate. The NSU trio: Uwe Mundlos, born 1973, member of the Thälmann Pioneers during the GDR days, later the FDJ, until 1989 student at the Magnus Poser polytechnic high school in Jena-Winzerla, hobby chemist, already a skinhead before 1989, from 1991 radicalized in the Jena neo-Nazi scene, whose ideas held sway among the young people in the city from late 1993. Uwe Böhnhardt, born 1977, Pioneer and member of the FDJ, grew up in the housing estates of Neulobeda-Ost, already a criminal and right-wing radical as a teenager, in 1988 the death of his older brother in an accident, after 1990 extreme right-wing skinhead with contacts to the Thuringia NPD,[1] after 1990 prosecuted five times for various criminal offences, member of the radical right-wing organization Thüringer Heimatschutz and Kameradschaft Jena. Beate Zschäpe, born 1975, unknown father of Romanian origin, childhood frequently in the care of her grandmother, mother divorced twice, six moves in Jena

[1] National Democratic Party, a far-right, ultranationalist neo-Nazi political party.

before she was fifteen, after 1990 painter's assistant and gar-
dener's apprentice. Initially a member of the left-wing Jena
punk scene but in 1990 also joined the militant Kameradschaft
Jena after meeting Uwe Mundlos.

Three unification children from Jena, socialized in eroded
GDR families and eroded GDR schools, in a political and
cultural shredder culture, more precisely in a shadow area
of society. Growing up in a vacuum, without attachments,
without empathy, without attention. Validated, supported
and protected only by an increasingly radicalized right-wing
scene in Thuringia's post-1990 political vacuum. That has also
been written about. But are these the reasons for killing? Three
young East Germans, travelling from the year 2000 around
the unified country and killing on racist grounds, turning up,
executing and disappearing, without words, as if there was in
any case nothing more to say. The brutality of their deeds is
unarguable. It formed a crack in the political tectonics of our
country. Did it also change it?

TRANSMISSIONS. The lust for violence in the East and
the unification children as the amok generation, the third
armoured generation. Once again, in his essay 'Morden für
das vierte Reich' [Killing for the Fourth Reich], Jan Lohl
analyses the 'logic of the derealization of the past' and notes
'that the phantom effect does not weaken over the generations'. The reality content of the phantom cannot be checked
across the generations but must be made to disappear. For the
fragmented memory of East Germany – and not only for the
great-grandchildren generation – this is an internal mental
process that has been given too little attention to date. Even
more important, the historic upheaval of 1989 could well have
reinforced the phantom effects still further.

More than fifty years' experience of dictatorship – ruptures,
taboos, traumas, continuities, burdens, the stories of victims,
perpetrators and fellow travellers – all this needed to be

integrated not only into the story of the East German identity but also into family biographies. A weight that after 1989
seemed to admit only a haptic relationship to history. This
was a society facing an unordered, repeatedly hushed-up and
completely distorted lump of history but also an inherited
portfolio which it rummaged in, felt its way around and regis-
tered seismographically, and which, often enough, also led to
detachment and mental paralysis. Endless reports in the media
about abuse of office, corruption and the Stasi that appeared
arbitrary and agenda-driven. Who was to be believed? What
was true and what was false? The third East German generation wanted a clean sheet, an unwritten wall, the whiteness
of a beginning, and was confronted instead by disoriented,
mostly compromised parents, untrustworthy teachers, the loss
of the familiar. People lived as if in a vacuum, with no tools, no
security, no ideals. What could this generation fall back on?
What would prove sustainable?

The static GDR society in its death throes: an increasing
number of war grandchildren had harked back to the grandiose self-image of their real or chosen grandparents and joined
forces in skinhead, hooligan or neo-Nazi groups to commit
acts of violence. The 'heroic struggle', the 'sacred earth', the
'iron rations' – these images made it appear possible to pre-
serve an ideal, often by attempting to set the family memory
against the Communist state memory. This persistent recourse
to the destructive grandiose self-image of the war generation
ultimately underwent a further shift in the political wasteland
of the east of Germany after 1989. The psychoanalyst Arno
Gruen spoke of a 'latent displaceable hate', which was once
again transposed, in view of the new need to derealize a dual
past – both National Socialism and the SED dictatorship. But
also because after 1990 the east of Germany gradually became
a testing ground for right-wing ideologies. Thus, from the
mid-1990s members of the NPD were elected for ten years to
the state governments of Saxony and Mecklenburg-Western

Pomerania. The DVU[2] was in parliament for a decade in Brandenburg and for a legislative period in Saxony-Anhalt. According to official figures from the Ministry of the Interior, after unification there were three times as many prosecutions for neo-Nazi or racially motivated offences in proportion to the population in the East as there were in the West. Jan Lohl points out that in spite of different historical experiences, generations were able to live in an 'imaginary shared past'. They confuse past and present, act as if Nazism was never defeated and transfer the 'present Federal Republic to the past Third Reich, which is once again elevated to become the ideal for the future. This also applied to the NSU murderers.'

New times, new actors, new media, which also opened up new referential spaces, particularly after the Columbine attack in the USA in 1999. The virtual world acted as an amplifier, a space for learning, play and dissimulation. In it, the loser mentality was transformed into one of omnipotence: we are the redeemers and we are allowed – indeed obliged – to kill. The attraction of the extreme, the determination to commit violence, the hubris of terror, all of this could be learnt and rehearsed in the virtual world. The school of killing as a self-confirming, self-learning system. Historical schools of destruction – Nazism being a strikingly frequent example – are linked to contemporary ones. The future act of killing is also fed by images. The killer trio in Jena who, from their hiding place in Chemnitz, enthusiastically followed the collapse of the Twin Towers in New York on TV. And who in their notorious acknowledgement video portrayed the Pink Panther as a 'nationalist at work', a figure on a 'tour of Germany' with the mission, apparently, to appear from nowhere to strike. No traces, no clues, no associations, no context. The Pink Panther as a mobile killing force with a partisan strategy that saw itself as somehow vastly superior to the authorities. Not only killing

[2] German People's Union, a far-right party.

its victims but mocking them sadistically as well. The new National Socialism – as an unassailable terrorist operation, as a nightmare in which the only ones laughing were those with the pistols, bombs and rifles.

NAUTILUS

Robby comes running up the stairs, groaning a bit: god-awful, the autobahn again. Endless traffic jams. But come on, I want to show you something.

Where are you going?

I'm not telling you. Come on, let's go.

We travel to Berlin Zoo. He points to the aquarium house on the right. He wants to take photos for his new exhibition. What's it about? I ask. He looks at me out of the corner of his eye. Symbioses, he says, but I need more material.

Here, in the aquarium?

Why not?

The crocodile hall, the snakes, lizards, caimans, rays. Robby points to a three-metre-long glass case. That's what I was looking for. Lizards and scorpions.

Why them?

Because they all crawl together into the same hole in the desert at night.

I watch my brother, how he chooses his subjects, how he moves, walks, looks. There's something different, I think.

Hey, are you seeing someone? I ask. He carries on taking photos, stops in front of two lizards, circles me, smiles dreamily.

They look geared up for war, I say, and point to the armoured creatures.

But they're completely harmless, says Robby with a wave of the hand. Herbivores, all of them.

We keep going. Wow, he says, amazed. In front of us is a large coral reef. That's it! – A symbiosis? – All the things growing there in the sea and transforming into islands and atolls, they are all animals. The coral has quite a complicated relationship with the algae, but they only have one thing in mind, which is to cooperate. Otherwise they'll die. Again the camera clicks. Shrimps, lichens, anemones. Once the symbiosis starts, there's no holding back anymore. Robby quickly takes the pictures he needs. We wander aimlessly along the glass cases and then stop in front of a dark expanse of water, which flashes from time to time. My brother reads out from the label next to the case: a nautilus lives on the steep sides of the Pacific coral reefs, at a depth of 300 to 400 metres during the day. It's a relic of long bygone days, with a twisted chalk shell, which protects its soft body and into which it can retract. A nautilus has a pinhole-camera eye and can put out the light when it is threatened by turning the eye around on its axis and looking inward until the attacker goes away. At night, when it has to come up to look for food, it can split its eye and look up and down at the same time.

Skins of consciousness

OPENINGS. 'I think my life is just beginning. At the moment I'm trying as best I can to get my school-leaving certificate. I was hoping to study computer science, but I need ten points in my special subject, which I won't get. So I have unfortunately had to give up this dream.' Sentences from a year 11 German essay. They are clear and straightforward. Two years later, the author Robert Steinhäuser, born 1983, would shoot sixteen people and then himself at his former school, the Gutenberg-Gymnasium in Erfurt. The sociologist Wilhelm Heitmeyer calls the years after 2000 the 'unsecured decade'.

26 April 2002. The first school shooting spree in Germany, public killings by a secondary school pupil. Unimaginable. Where you were when you heard this news is wedged in your memory. The place, the time, the people you were with, their looks, their reactions. I think of Inga and Thomas, Hanna, Svenja, Stephan, who did their leaving certificate at this school and today need little prompting to start talking about what was torn open and revealed, what could no longer be concealed, what never felt right again. An initial shock. 'No one talks,' says Inga, 'but the wall, the dark wall remains. As if we lived in a soundproofed room. Nothing has been sorted out, nothing has

become clearer since.' – 'Amok,' says Hanna, 'is the only subject that has to do with our generation. 'It's our thing. Erfurt
was a rupture. After that, something new began.'

'Socialization takes place through violence,' writes Klaus
Theweleit. As if Robert Steinhäuser had shot into the belly of
the East. The reaction that followed the killing was a disaster,
a political disaster, a media information disaster. A disaster in
waves that should have been analysed in the rear-view mirror
of German history. Post-dictatorship Thuringia after 1989
would have been an ideal blueprint. Nothing was done. There
was no political will and also no formats for such an analysis.
But there was still the question of who was in charge there in
the mid-1990s. What was going on? Who failed to spot the
NSU, which had established itself so easily in Thuringia years
before the shooting rampage in Erfurt? Is there a connection?

Looking for an answer, the same names crop up again and
again: first ministers, ministers of the interior, ministers of justice, mayors. West and East Germans. War children, post-war
children, Wall children, who in all the rebuilding managed one
thing in particular after 1990: the establishment of a bizarre and
special form of democracy. One political thriller after the other.
And they all remained unsolved. What looked initially through
1989 in Thuringia like a fresh start had transformed the state
more and more into a political and mental borderland, with
a public sphere that was clogged up without any real sound-
ing board for an exchange of ideas. Mysterious mega-deals in
the catering and housing sectors were everyday occurrences.
Erfurt was booming and could be invested in without risk.

In his book *Ermitteln verboten!* the journalist Jürgen Roth
writes about the Italian Mafia and the Calabrian 'Ndrangheta,
which from the 1990s were looking for new areas in which
to operate and incorporated Eastern Europe into their trans-
national networks. The new federal states were virgin territory
for this kind of business, strategically well placed and therefore
hugely profitable. Thanks to its central location, Thuringia

– and above all Erfurt – became important investment bases. The Mafia practice of laying false trails took hold there without any resistance. The criminal family business from San Luca, at the time with an annual worldwide revenue of 44 billion euros, invested and laundered money, above all in the catering trade, in the housing market, and in the trafficking of arms, drugs and human beings.

For a lot of political decision-makers, the south Italian operations appeared profitable, not just at the level of regional policy but above all in local government. Those at the top were able to live well in the land of accomplices. People knew what was going on, noted the special interests of the other party and looked away. Unification funds at the time were there for the taking, there was an endless amount of rebuilding to do, and the *modus vivendi* was a kind of stabilizing consensus politics aimed solely at consolidating this special form of regionalism. That's what happened in Thuringia, but also in Saxony, where two CDU first ministers reigned for eleven and twelve years, respectively. The two have yet to provide answers as to why their states formed the basis for the emergence of right-wing extremism and how the connection between Jena and the NSU, Erfurt and Chemnitz worked.

After the shooting rampage at the Gutenberg-Gymnasium in 2002, the mood in Thuringia was heated and highly agitated. People had imagined that the time after 1989 would be different. Mafia, investment bubbles, red light stories involving the police, corruption? They'd had enough, and wanted the truth to come out The regional media had endless material: 'If Thuringian politics doesn't put an end to all this favouritism, it will soon be in for a surprise.' – 'What a self-service store!' – 'Time to change, enough of these perks!' Public criticism was unusually harsh.

TENTACLES. Catch-up reality checks that took place again and again in the east of Germany after 1989. The Erfurt rampage was called a watershed, but then there was the next one. In retrospect it looks like a series, of new, interruptive, explosive, disturbing, usually cryptic hidden objects: the curb stomping in Potzlow in 2002,[1] the murder of Enrico Schreiber in Frankfurt/Oder in 2003, the nine dead babies in Brieskow-Finkenherd in 2005,[2] the burning to death of Oury Jalloh in Dessau prison, also in 2005. Hate acts – excessive ones in some cases – that are part of the story of East Germany's implosive history. As if a struggle were taking place within the trauma, in a destructive force field that revealed the hatred implanted in an enclosed society but which could not escape it.

Three days after Robert Steinhäuser's rampage, Inga, Thomas and I travelled to Erfurt. The two were studying at the Berlin drama school, the 'Busch', and were in my art of poetry course. Now they felt the need to see their old teachers, to be in the city and to meet friends. It was late April and cold. I recall crowded apartments, pitch-black wet streets, shocked and wide-eyed faces. I recall something massive. As if in just a few hours we had slipped down a level in our lives and landed in a place where other laws applied. I remember how we smoked like crazy, drank absurd concoctions and didn't sleep. And that for a time there was no stopping it. Then came the call.

It was about father. A journalist introduced himself, said what he was working on and what he had discovered. He spoke of a file he had asked to see and which had remained initially for months in the Ministry of the Interior. Now he had it and had looked at it. He asked what I thought of it. What are you talking about? I heard myself say. He started over. He spoke softly but in my ears his words sounded aggressive. I didn't want to hear them, I didn't want to answer him, I didn't want

---

[1] Torture and murder by three neo-Nazis of sixteen-year-old Marinus Schöberl.

[2] Nine newborn babies were found dead in the garden of a house in Brieskow near the Polish border. They had been murdered by their mother.

to be dragged into something that I had enough difficulty anyway in keeping at arm's length. I hung up. He rang right back. I could read you the file, he said. I'll think about it, I said and pushed his voice away. I felt as if I was being snooped on. Something was getting too near to me.

The words stay with me, and I think once again about my transitional phase, the cotton wool years after 1989, the many loose ends and a diffuse feeling that I couldn't grasp. As if life had no beginning, no middle. But now perhaps? I needed to speak with Robby. He also needed to know about it. I didn't call him but drove to Berlin. I wanted to read father's file. Hundreds of reports, in his hard, sprawling handwriting. The first pages made me feel jealous: I would so much have liked to receive a letter from him. 'My daughter, we were in the woods today and picked blackberries. On the way back I carried you on my shoulders, and you fell asleep. Your stockings tickled my neck. I'll have to buy you some new ones tomorrow.' Something like that. After a hundred pages I fought against my excitement: so that's what happens to a terrorist agent in the Black Forest who slips down into a field because the snow plough hasn't come. After two hundred pages there was disgust, after three hundred a feeling of being unhoused.

The memory machine in my head. The missing jigsaw puzzle pieces. The words in the files. The dates and alibi dates, the addresses and alibi addresses, the missions and places, the expenses and leftover amounts. 'Expense account for the mission from 15 to 18 December 1973 in Marburg/Lahn. Received 900 West marks on account, total expenditure DM863.78. Gerhard.' The woollen scarf that mother loved so much and that had cost DM29.50 in Marburg. Father's leather cap that lay for years on top of the wardrobe and is booked on the sheet as costing DM37.95. I tried to interpret the numbers and words. The empty spaces felt like black ice. I was getting closer and closer to what I was looking for. Soon it would be there. I tried not to imagine what happened on 19 December 1973.

I was relieved that there was no mention of it. I have to call Robby. Right away.

Years later at an exhibition at the Fraunhofer Institute I saw a kind of file washing-machine, where all kinds of snippets were put in at one end, which then sought each other, as if fitted with tentacles, whirling, jumping, dancing, until the bits that had originally belonged together found each other again. The busy searching noise, which made me feel that there would be a happy ending. I dialled Robby's number. I had jotted down notes on father's file. I wanted to be as precise as possible. I wanted to give my brother an idea. I started slowly. Then I told him about father's Marburg mission. He knew straightaway what I was talking about. He described how father had come home, sat down at the kitchen table, and what happened next. We tried to sort and put things in the right order. We still didn't have any words but got the general shape of things. Something that had lived within us. I said: It just happened. It had no meaning. We had nothing to do with it. Robby said nothing. Why don't you say anything? I asked. It's no good, I can't, he answered.

ECHO SOUNDER. After 1989, the political resolution was not to lose valuable time and to do better than after the first dictatorship. The GDR crimes needed to be prosecuted as fully as possible. The conditions didn't seem so bad: detailed investigations, committed jurists, political will. And yet there was more talking about it than actual results. The underlying principle was that if in doubt find for the defendant. The accused knew that they had this advantage, there was no trace of victor's justice. At 11.59 p.m. on 2 October 2000, the political tectonics of the East once again shifted discernibly, though it was barely noticed. Thereafter, the legal investigation of the GDR ceased, and all crimes except for murder were subject to the statute of limitations. As if someone had secretly pressed the reset button.

The 2000s as the leaden time in the east of Germany. The system had had its leadership cut off, but the GDR continued to exist as an enclave structure: in the work of the state parliaments and local councils of Perleberg or Ilmenau, in the elite and memory culture and the public sector, in the media, in sport. There were regional differences, sometimes considerable. In Saxony, for example, all teachers who had only taught civics were dismissed. But continuity regained the upper hand. 'No state dismissed more than half of the unmasked Stasi informers in the public sector,' wrote Grit Hartmann and Uwe Müller in their investigative analysis *Vorwärts und vergessen!* twenty years after the fall of the Berlin Wall. The secret service in the Saxon police departments, at the MDR, in the Brandenburg parliament. In Cottbus, formerly the district with the greatest proportion of Stasi informers, an eminent network of companies dominated the municipal building sector. 'Partners were often the wives of the managing directors of municipal companies and former full-time Stasi employees,' wrote Hartmann and Müller. The state of the media also influenced the political climate. 'After 1989, journalists managed to continue unchallenged to an extent greater than practically any other professional group in the east of Germany.' At the beginning of 2000, 60 per cent of them were still employed by the former regional party newspapers, whose circulation remained consistently high.

It was made easy for the well-educated, pragmatic but incriminated elite in the east of Germany – in business, the public sector, politics and the media – to feather their nests without hindrance. Until 3 October 2000, they knew to say nothing, and after that they went about occupying strategic positions, working on their own careers and trying to make sure that they couldn't be dismissed. They knew what to do if something was revealed or rather how much they should admit and when it was wiser to keep quiet again. Apart from that they were interested in exploiting all the advantages

of a society that until 1989 they had systematically tried
to abolish.

The 2000s. Apart from outward reconstruction, consolidation and building boom, according to statistics in the
post-dictatorship East, it was a time of rapidly increasing
violence and rising child poverty. There were three times
the number of domestic murders, and first drug experiences by juveniles started four years earlier than in the West.
Dislocation, denial, non-delivery. The trauma of the East collided with the trauma of insecurity. In 2004 my book about
the shooting rampage in Erfurt appeared. For a year I drove
around the east of the country. In Dresden an old woman
asked me what I would do if everything changed again. It was
not until a good ten years later that I understood the question.
In Gera a man sitting on the back row shouted that he would
scream if I said something critical about the GDR. In Rostock
a woman explained that she would get on best with the Scots.
Why? – Because they are occupied like we are.

After the readings came the random reports: the man whose
childhood was without doorknobs. He spent his first years in
a Stasi children's brothel. He can't sleep. The girl who as an
eight-year-old diver was afraid to do a somersault, was tied up
repeatedly, sank like a stone in the water and was then fished
out by someone. She can't sleep either. The insomniacs who
find no peace because they are not heard and feel unaccepted,
ignored, blanked out, discarded. I think of the echo sounder of
pain that won't go away. Where should it go to? I think of how
they stand before me and say nothing, how it starts again, how
they look at me and go away because I'm not the right one, just
a disappointment. I think of all the prohibitions to which the
insomniacs are exposed all the time, the ever-louder words:
'You have to learn to look forward.' – 'We should pay more
attention to the grey areas of the dictatorship.' – 'It's about time
we put all this behind us.' – 'And why have you still not become
reconciled?' – 'It's time to take a lighter touch with history.'

ON ICE. In 1989, the West quietly transferred the Holocaust as a key aspect of identity, as a European myth of barbarity, but also of suffering, to the East. It became the central focus of the public policy of the new unified Germany, secured by the cornerstones of constitutional patriotism and anti-totalitarian consensus. This was by no means as obvious as it seemed at the time of unification. Over a period of forty years and in the most painstaking mini-steps, with scandals, harsh controversies, exhibition fights, denials and many historical political volte-faces, the West had talked itself out of the default self-image as a perpetrator society towards a collective policy of memory, ultimately declaring the commemoration of the victims to be inviolable. An endless zigzag between suppression, management and renunciation. The burden of guilt of National Socialism sat too painfully and too shamefully on society and in families. For far too long West Germany had feverishly attempted, as the literary scholar and essayist Karl-Heinz Bohrer put it, to normalize what cannot be normalized. There were constant discussions, articles and actions aimed at disconnecting the guilt. Ultimately and at around the same time as the fall of the Berlin Wall, a complicated structure formed – an attitude that combined routine, deliberate disruption, frivolity, serious memory politics and moralizing – that Bohrer called 'the second skin of the West German conscience'. It was based on the premise: 'Good has prevailed, evil has been banished.'

The West never spoke with the East about this decision, never wanted to speak about it and was probably not able to. The Day of German Unity made this sacrosanct and provided the necessary direction on the journey to a self-assured nation. A status quo, an ineluctable requirement. In the turmoil of the time, the fact that this would pose massive problems for the eastern part of the country was inevitably ignored. Moreover, in this self-image, two contrasting political myths also collided.

On the one hand, the West – after a slow start but then systematically from the 1970s onwards – had opened itself up to the history of the victims, but then after 1989 all the more systematically styled itself as a victim of the Hitler system. It had worked hard on itself, gone the whole distance with the guilt question, and the various actors were now snuggling up politically in a mood of relaxed reconciliation. 'While some new books are devoted to the perpetrators of the Nazi regime, down to the simple soldier and citizen, others take a nuanced view of the suffering of the German people. The origins of German antisemitism, the thoughts of the soldiers, the mentality of the German generals on the one hand, the German prisoners of the SS, the fate of post-war children with their soldier fathers, suicide in the Third Reich or the illusion of coming to terms with the past to become perceived as victims on the other. The German victims have long joined ranks with the German perpetrators, the view has become more open,' wrote Lukas Hammerstein in *Die Guten und das Böse*.

However, this more open view ignored the unbridgeable gap between victim and perpetrator memories. Moreover, the East had no say in the new memory politics of the unified Germany. In all subsequent discussion, and there was a considerable amount – be it Spielberg's film *Schindler's List* in 1993, the Wehrmacht exhibition from 1995, Martin Walser's speech in 1998,[3] or the admission by the late Günter Grass in 2006[4] – the perspective of the former East Germany was non-existent. There wasn't one. Did anyone notice this in the heat of the battle? Probably not. The discussion was much too controversial; much too much unsecured terrain had to be marked out. Despite the nicest summer's tales,[5] relationships within Germany were too fragile and under considerable tension.

[3] In this controversial speech, Walser, a German author, criticized the culture of perpetual guilt and victimhood associated with the Holocaust.
[4] Admission that the German novelist had been a member of the Waffen-SS.
[5] Reference to the documentary film *Deutschland: Ein Sommermärchen* by Sönke Wortmann about the FIFA World Cup in Germany in 1996 and the sense of unity and pan-German national pride it was said to generate.

The East had no preparation or footing in this furious debate about Nazi history. Through the Buchenwald doctrine, the single government party had effectively exonerated the East Germans and turned them into a victim society pure and simple. In the GDR, fascism was deemed to have been expunged, the major war criminals punished, the institutions denazified, the economy nationalized, the nobility ousted and the remaining Nazis all hiding out in the West. The GDR refused to pay reparations claimed by Israel for Holocaust victims and as early as 1953 described them as 'out-and-out agitation'. A period of anti-Jewish psychosis. In spite of tough negotiations in the background, this hard-hearted refusal to accept any responsibility remained unchanged until the end of the system. In the East, the Jewish Claims Conference banged its head against a brick wall.

The West justifiably claimed to have led the way in the inescapable question of responsibility for the victims. The East styled itself as a victim society, in which the Holocaust was put on ice. Unexplained, unspoken, unmastered. Two political myths, two skins of consciousness that were non-transferable, incompatible. How would that work? Following on from the initial celebration, unification pride and goodwill, the East fell back after 1990 into its trance-like role, in an immaterial existential envy that was possibly more significant than any-thing that had to do with money, the fire sale of state assets, pensions or material legacy. In the academic world, in schools and in public, the east of Germany – which always considered its society to have more solidarity than the West and to be a stronghold of warmth, help, cooperation – extensively blanked out the persecution and murder of six million Jews and in fact never even considered it seriously. Most of the public are still unaware of it today. How is this to be explained?

BRIGHT SURFACES

Robby and I are cycling on the Elbe, first on bumpy cobble-stones, then on gravel with sand squishing in between. We are on our way to Laubegast. Melli Beese, the first German woman pilot, was born there. I want to write about flying. I've wanted to do so for some time, but something was missing. Laubegast, where the river makes a sharp bend and the fat Elbe seagulls flop onto the water. The Storchennest and Donaths Neue Welt, the dance hall from Beese's time. We watch the seagulls as they tell each other their stories – about the cable ferry, the floods, the Molkerei Naake and the old wharf. We imagine the sharpening of steel blades, the busy cries of the workers. We see the slow-flowing Elbe, the hollows and the overgrown embankments. It's nice here, says my brother. Yes, it is.

We could continue, but we stop by the river. We sit down on the pebbled banks. They are warm and dry. Robby asks if I remember our spaceships in the garden, the masses of woodlice, and Eagle 1. Do you remember how it goes? he asks. Let me have a try, I reply. I release the brake, push the throttle as far as it will go, grab the joystick, pretend that we are being pressed into the back of our seats. The river gurgles. Ready for take-off? I ask. Ready for take-off, he confirms, in his commander's voice. The sound of the engine revving. We lift off. Follow the dotted line, then the wide bend through all the happy spots, I hear him next to me. Make sure not to lose altitude. The fat seagulls are now next to us. Their screeching. How they glide softly on the water as if it were a large unmoving field. How do they fly so high when they're so fat? Is it true that they can fly round the world? Robby talks of their routes to the Equator. I wonder what it's like to be a seagull, I say, pointing to the wisps of cloud. My brother becomes serious, weaves in and out, presses and squeezes his way through the air, and then soars up above. He's talking about flying.

How the seagulls sweep over the Elbe. They soar and dive down, untroubled by anything. In their eyes, the river, upside down, and so small that it looks as if it could be emptied out in one go. What remains, what memory, what words, what smells? Highest heights? Deepest depths? The machine picks up speed. We fly over the Weisser Hirsch. Robby points down. Our childhood, San Remo, the Luisenhof, the yellow gondolas. The heath right at the side of the road. Lots of dense woods. They glisten and smell of stillness. My brother sets the chronometer, calculates the speed, his hands moving automatically, as if we'd been flying like that all our lives. He points down again. The Waldschlösschen, the Frauenkirche, the Semper opera, the Zwinger. We see people sitting in front of cafés, unloading their shopping from their cars, standing on the street and talking. Robby takes off his pilot's goggles, rubs his nose. In front of us the seagulls, swooping from the sky, through the gathering clouds.

We are in the air. We feel safe. Nothing can touch us. It's not easy to write about flying.

Unification Nirvana

SPLITTING SYNDROME. The political coordinates in our country, its political face, have changed markedly since summer 2015. We are in a new situation, some say in another society. Is this some special kind of nervousness, the latest version of German angst, or already the dismantling of the system? At any event, the discourse has shifted clearly to the right, and a turning point has been reached. With Pegida[1] and a strong AfD,[2] political consensus now hangs demonstrably in the balance. Right-wing revolt, disruptive politics, the splitting of the republic, a phalanx for the *reconquista*, the reconquering of Europe – all these terms try to describe how Germany was in stress-test mode, fighting for political answers. And on that score, time was running out: European elections in May 2019, regional elections in Saxony and Brandenburg in September 2019 and seven weeks later in Thuringia, the next federal elections in 2021. People were already talking of a watershed moment. Germany was under pressure. At the same time, the

---

[1] Patriotic Europeans Against the Islamization of the West, a pan-European, anti-Islam, far-right political movement.
[2] Alternative for Germany, a right-wing populist political party.

situation was paradoxical. The better the figures, the more the government in Berlin proudly and confidently emphasized what it had achieved, the more uneasy and gloomy the feeling was in the country at large. The ground was shaky. The situation was at odds with the mood. The splitting syndrome needed to be revisited: in both the East and the West people knew again what was good and what was evil.

The first comments on the results of the 2017 federal elections sounded as if they had been prepared in advance. 'What do you expect? The people in the East can't keep up, they can't handle the change.' The talk was mostly of differences in pay and pensions compared with the West, the lack of social security and the inheritance that failed to materialize. It was about money. Slotted into talk shows perhaps as fillers. We hear it, but with a feeling that something else is shaping the political reality in the East. There is a distinct gap, something worryingly elusive that remains unsaid, between what we have concocted looking back over the years and the German rhinoceros that has entered the Bundestag. What is it?

The war grandchildren of East Germany. If I look closely at the figures from the last federal elections for Saxony alone, where 27 per cent voted for the AfD, the typical new right-wing voter appears to be male, between 50 and 65 years old. The kind of man who wants to restrict immigration, is more than averagely proud of his Saxon origins and cannot get to grips with his fear of serious crime. I want to take the figures seriously. I spent my childhood in Dresden on the Weisser Hirsch with boys in my class who want one thing above all today: to close the borders, feed their anger, break taboos. I look today at our school desks back then, from Steffen to Hans, with Marion sitting between, to Peter, Hendrik and Tobias. I can see their bright, alert faces as if no time has passed between our schooldays and today. We were never like that, I say immediately and am quite sure of it. How could we have been? Children don't close themselves off, they want to discover the world. Our childhood was small, but we imagined it as being immense.

And of course today we don't want to hear any more about absent people, about taboos, silent fathers and grandfathers, the guilt dynamic in post-war families in both East and West. We say we know all that, we're tired of it, we've had enough. The bookshelves are overflowing, the films have been made. We know everything we have to know. And anyway the times have changed. And now? The AfD focuses on Germany, *heimat*, identity. It is the party for the insecure, the political meltdown which it claims is good for the country. But which Germany, which *heimat*, which identity?

SOLDIERS OF GOOD FORTUNE. I think of Michael, born in 1966, whom I met at university in Jena. A political thinker, good with words, critical of the system, defiant and adaptable. It was not long before he joined the student opposition. He was kicked out, had to leave the university and go to work. After 1989 he remained in Thuringia, got involved in the cultural scene, organized exhibitions, obtained public funding for major projects. He did what he had always wanted to do. But Thuringia was Thuringia, just like Saxony was Saxony and Brandenburg Brandenburg. Outwardly they projected an image of progressive reconstruction but inwardly they remained without a solid foundation. Confusion and disillusionment were widespread. Political standards were non-existent and were neither introduced nor demanded. There was no credible processing of the GDR crimes. Everyone could take it as they wished. Victims? Never saw any. Perpetrators? No idea.

Michael was working in Erfurt at the time when Robert Steinhäuser went on his rampage at the Gutenberg-Gymnasium. He was living in a city in shock that seemed to shut itself off like a stronghold. For him it was a picture of what was to come. In the West the dominant narrative was of war fathers and war mothers, war children and war grandchildren.

In the East the GDR became increasingly untouchable. GDR museums shot up from the ground like mushrooms. GDR myths like the Buchenwald inmate and author Bruno Apitz, the Peace Race[3] hero Täve Schur or the writer Maxie Wander[4] were publicly and consistently defended with great passion, without regard for the facts and documents about them produced by dedicated historical researchers after 1989, or for the historical ambivalence they suggested. In essence, historical truth rolls off the GDR like water off a duck's back. How can a clear picture of the path to democracy be achieved under such circumstances? Who defines the guiding principles? What is relevant, how much of the underlying foundations has to be confirmed, and whose biographies should be revealed? What principles should have guided the East during the years when its political and emotional life was uprooted?

Michael, meanwhile, began to read every book about Hitler and embrace conspiracy theories. He had no luck with women, lost his money on the stock exchange and became a media junkie. When I drove from Darmstadt to Berlin in 1996, I sometimes passed through Erfurt and would meet him in the Speicher where we would talk about our new lives. At some point he moved to the capital for work. We met regularly there. Michael, the good guy, who always listened and understood, until understanding became difficult. When Angela Merkel changed the country in 2015 with her refugee policy, he turned to the AfD and became a close collaborator of Alexander Gauland.

Looking back today, I would have to say that in summer 2015, Angela Merkel and her slogan 'Wir schaffen das!' ('We can do it!') basically broke up my old circle of friends from the East. That's a terrible thing to say, and on the face of it,

---

[3] Eastern European cycling race.
[4] Author of *Guten Morgen, Du Schöne* about the daily life of women in East Germany.

it's not right either. But still, it's true that we haven't been friends since summer 2015. For a while we would meet on the street and argue with each other about the refugees. Although, or even because, the friends themselves came from refugee families. Although after the Second World War, East Germany became a permanent refugee society. The millions who came? The millions who left? When it became clear that it wasn't about refugees but about who we are, what we want here and now, what we really live for, what is really important to us, we stopped talking. This silence persists. I can't be sure that I am right in this conflict. I can't even be sure that I basically understood what has separated us so decisively. I only know that it happened. It's about ties that existed throughout the dictatorship period and that, as I thought, couldn't be broken. But that's what happened. We have become fundamentally different and are now so far apart that we can no longer consider ourselves friends. But what was it that we didn't want to see although it was apparently quite evident for a long time? When did the AfD, as we call it today, start to come between us? What took shape, what changed, in the shadow of politics after 1989?

STANDBY. The war grandchildren as the undead of the war. We as the Wall generation who no longer believed in any ideology. Who grew up without a fatherland and mother tongue, as Heiner Müller once said. Who in 1989 suddenly had a whole world before us and carried in ourselves the lost political mandate as cheerful promoters of the red system. Who managed to get by for better or worse after 1989. And a growing number of whom today pursue a two-front strategy. I think, as in childhood, with a closed visor, armoured and masked. Today, to vote AfD is not a soapbox protest but has long been a clear belief: the world, and Germany in particular, runs better and more unambiguously when Philistines like us are also finally in power.

The war children, the war grandchildren and their shared history of a hidden war that covered up the violence externally while internalizing it and living it out in a narrow-minded, fascistoid GDR, and absorbing it to the point of total denial and even extinction. The Wall generation, the last one to have an emotional connection with the past extreme century and today the core AfD voters. It goes together. It can be seen in the body language, in the untended emotional wounds, in the traumatic memory of a generation, in the quicksand of family loyalties or also in the unsuccessful attempt to deal with the phantoms. The baby boomers of the East, the war grandchildren, or how soldiers of good fortune were transformed into soldiers of hate. The fact that this generation's political mandate was not one that it ever accepted of its own accord also plays a role here. They wanted to escape from the collective GDR we-identity and the promised land imposed on them and fled in large numbers to the West via Prague or Budapest when the chance first presented itself in summer 1989. And then?

When the Berlin Wall fell, it was time for a new start. But the East German war grandchildren were not shot at by the tyrants in their own country like their peers elsewhere, on the Maidan in Kyiv or Tahrir Square in Cairo. They were not obliged, like their peers from Eastern Europe, to accept the most menial jobs in London or Paris so as to feed their families in Poland or Bulgaria. They were well-off thanks to the unexpected historical good fortune of the century. Young enough to start over; old enough to rely on their experience. Their political mandate had been pulverized overnight by the peaceful revolution. For the vocal 'no' and longing for destruction of the core AfD voters in the east of Germany today, the political mandate snatched from them in 1989 now appears like a key moment. A generation primed for action remains on standby: it has been shaped. History has relieved them of their original assignment; the second assignment had better work.

PROMOTION. This middle-class clientele from the east of Germany would never have made it to the AfD, however, if the unification children had not come after them. The younger ones, who acted as ice breakers, who gave up the façade and have provided the older ones in recent years with the political room for action. Ones like Pegida founder Lutz Bachmann, born in Dresden in 1973, the former AfD politician Frauke Petry, born in Dresden in 1975, André Poggenburg, born in Weissenfels in 1975 and from 2014 to 2018 AfD chairman in Saxony-Anhalt, Matthias Lieschke, born in Wittenberg in 1970 and since 2016 AfD member of the Saxony-Anhalt regional parliament, Holger Arppe, born in Rostock in 1973, who in summer 2017 shocked the country with his repulsive Facebook chats. A generational line that could be continued at will. They are the visible ones, the ones who can't be missed. Like every other generation, it is not homogeneous, but the words of those that are heard are remarkably similar: we have been attacked, we are the victims, we have to defend ourselves, we demand a patriotic counter-culture, an emancipation movement must be created. They want to be there, in public, visible. Power and careers are at stake. They are the vocal advocates gambling away the happiness capital of our democracy.

What Hitler's great-grandchildren like to forget are the gaping omissions in the story of East Germany. Their vanishing point is in the distance – Germany in the solid structure that has existed for the past 1,000 years. Just let's not be too specific. There is a lot to the AfD, just as there is with Pegida, the Identitarians, the Reichsbürger and the Deutsche Burschenschaft. There are countless reasons for indignation. But the striking motifs are fundamentalism, hubris and exclusion. The desire for disinhibition is a feature of unbounded totalitarianism. It needs no foundation. But it's not the same for a society. To that extent, the absence of an identity narrative for East Germany remains vitally relevant, as does its culture of hate. One thing is clear: no party in the new Germany has developed a programme or an idea to confront the lust for violence of the East. It has been blinked away by the unified collective for the sake of social peace – even though overt extremist acts have, if anything, become more common. In quantitative terms alone, they have been consistently three times as frequent as in the West since 1990. Fifty years of dictatorship cannot be overcome by pampering, regionalism and withdrawal from political life. Totalitarian systems take away the burden of responsibility. Directing the affective valence of denial onto a democratic path is quite simply a component of identity-building.

For a quarter of a century, memory, recollection and identity have been part of the basso continuo of the new Germany. 'Different combinations of recollection, knowledge, defence and their generational manifestations can be discerned,' wrote Werner Bohleber, explaining it against the background of the experience of his own generation of West German war children. He says that they 'grew up in the shadow of the self-deception of their parents, who defined themselves as victims. Their silence about their own involvement and the gaps in the family biographies produced a diffuse and sometimes distorted sense of reality' – one that generates a confused and hazy impression in their children.

THE SPELL. Robby is gone. He'd only just begun. I often forget that. My brother is part of me, he is where he always was in me. How can that change? The superfluous has become even more superfluous, the essential more essential, the questions remain. Questions that formed our quarrel. Naturally I have lots of pictures in my head about Robby. Pictures from our shared childhood, his military service, university, his life after 1989. Our conflict after the fall of the Berlin Wall was always about the same thing: forefathers or no forefathers, father or no father. SS, Stasi, violence, or no SS, no Stasi, no violence.

And our grandmothers, our mother? It was about interior spaces, about us.

'I like the fact that the text is contemporary but also timeless. At least it refrains from precise references. The characters don't have clear personalities. You have to create them yourself,' Robby wrote to me about my first novel. I agreed with him. The book was unfocused, faltering, a real debut novel, as if emerging from a hiding place. But I didn't have the confidence to do more. To think beyond the words. That's what everyone likes. But how to open them up? How someone can be so familiar to you but then at some point simply closes the door behind them. And what comes next is in fact already there. That's how it was with Robby. His response to the pain of his childhood was cheerfulness, lightness. Why not? He wanted to be light, to invent himself as he went along, or as he himself described his life plan: to deceive himself in a good way.

'Writing is trying out sentences to see what they might mean,' says P.F. Thomese in *Shadow Child*. Robby's words – how to write them down so that it is possible to understand what they mean? That thing he used to say about the trap. Why the restlessness, the uneasiness in him, why so constantly and so single-mindedly forwards? What did he feel was holding him back inside, as if there were a stowaway in his head? Sometimes I thought about a way, about something that would help to get us out together. Step by step. Then sometimes I saw us running around in a circle, always the same circle, as if we were under a spell. I got hold of Robby's boxes. In one of them are photos, in another our letters, in a third the presents he gave me. For example, the CD *Build a Rocket Boys!* by Elbow, his favourite band. A world of absinthe lounges, billiards, horses and snowboards, jokers and karaoke, mostly in abandoned factories. Soaring hymns, in which boys build their rockets, the mother doesn't sleep, air traffic is backed up, the singer has a baby, the relay baton is dropped and lippy kids play. Robby, the popper, had become a gentle rocker. The band from Manchester delivered sublime Britpop at its best. 'Do they know those days are golden?' sings Guy Garvey, a stocky, red-haired forty-year-old from working-class Manchester, who insists that life will turn out all right.

As I listen to Elbow, feeling as if I'm in a well-heated church, Robby's sentences become louder, harder in me, as if they were demanding something. 'I'm always in between the words, like I'm in between everything,' I read in one letter. 'It's all right for you. You are always outside.' In October 2012 I sent him the extract from grandfather's file with the order of furniture from the Riga ghetto. 'Terrible,' he replied succinctly, 'how far away and yet so close everything is. Perhaps we slept in those sheets or ate from a tablecloth from there.' When I obtained a copy of father's file in 2014, I asked him to read it. He never did. 'Why me?' he asked. 'Why should I struggle with it? Why do I have to clear up this stuff? I don't want to see it. I want to put it behind me. I still have my life. I'm always on the lookout for new solutions, and perhaps my suppressing things has a function that's not just negative.' Robby had begun to build a protective shield. Our silences became longer.

BLUE IN GREEN

6 December 2017. The phone call. I see myself sitting in the car. A mild, misty, late afternoon. I'm just coming back from the university. I hear a voice. A calm voice. The world in general seems collected. The cars, the light, the people at the crossings. I try to listen. Words are spoken. It's clear that they are trying to tell me something. The ice pick starts at the junction of Yorckstrasse and Mehringdamm. After that it won't stop going through my head. For a year in the car. I want to be alone, with Robby, I want to remember. Our Warsaw trip, for example. Take a jacket, he says, tomorrow is already November.

– When does the train leave? I ask. Not a train. – Then what? – Hitching. – Oh. – All that talking in the compartment, it simply tires me. You have to be able to concentrate. I want to show you something. Something about me. You should know it. – What? – Miles Davis. Live. That's what we're here for. It's going to be great.

We stand on the autobahn. A Polish lorry driver picks us up. From Berlin eastward. The sky gets bigger, the landscape lonelier, until Warsaw greets us with its mouldy façades. We've made it! Let's rock, my brother shouts. Our destination: the Congress Hall, a real Stalin dinosaur. We pass the checkpoint without problem. The building smells of cleaning agent and fish. The auditorium fills up. Above our heads a bunch of spotlights darting across the stage like flickering miners' lamps. On it a forest of stools, instruments, high-heeled microphones. Half an hour when nothing happens. No king, no other player up there. Perhaps he won't come at all, I say to Robby. He says nothing. The audience begins to get restless. The crowd an animal, as if crouching in a hole, patient, fearful. Suddenly, there it is, his trumpet. On its own. Gentle and resolute. A mating call. The sound defiant, vulnerable, not possible to shake off. And right behind the sounds, him, King Miles, stalking in from the right. He takes his huge sunglasses off, looks for a long time at the audience. His gaze, peering through the bright spotlights, as if he were looking for someone in the audience. No one there.

He puts the trumpet to his mouth. The music takes off, carries the audience with it, into a maelstrom, a dense jungle. Ten people on the stage. One powerful stream: glowing, solitary, confusing. The drum solo, the bass, the saxophone. Kenny Garrett, shouts Robby. He's not much older than we are. But in the centre the old man. He's in complete control. He provides the raw sound, before sitting back and letting the boys do their thing. Miles Davis stands with his back to the audience. He's trying to tell us something, says Robby. What? I ask.

It's 30 October 1988. The bass booms. We're sweating. Finally the climax, the turning point. The fans close up and roar as if liberated. My head bangs. His back? What's this about? What's he trying to tell us? Turn away? We should turn away, we should go? Is that what he means? The last trumpet blast. Then silence. Miles Davis leaves the stage. Something in me nods after his glittering back. The musicians pack their things. It's over.

Okay, old King. One more winter and then I'm off.

The East as a testing ground

OPPOSITION. Michael and our last encounter: when he told me that even during the GDR era he was against the system, the establishment, those up there. And that he therefore had to be against it again today. That one had to stay aware and that he could pride himself on always having been in the opposition. Words that I have recently encountered more frequently.

The dissident scene in East Germany and its great legacy. It was above all their courage that made possible the unification of the country. Resistance that became a central element of pan-German history. At the same time it is paradoxical that this dissident scene did not basically become a public issue until parts of it drifted to the right in the refugee summer of 2015. For a long time people had overlooked the fact that the opposition in the GDR was quite disparate and had fed off the most diverse ideas and experiences, and that it also went very different ways after 1989. I realize that I'm on shaky ground here. It's not about discrediting the courageous. It's about asking once again what resistance in a dictatorship does with its protagonists, what the precise targeting of brutality by the system meant, what *Zersetzung* and isolation are and what they caused. Political dissidence in East Germany also meant 300,000 political prisoners – 300,000 people and their families, their friends, their lives. Even after 1989, this story remained one of the nightmares that was carried over, one of almost unresolvable anxiety-filled spaces, the guilt forced into the bodies, not justified but also not easy to shake off.

Dissidence in East Germany: politically it had nowhere to go after 1989. Who was interested in it? It had no lobby, its experience was given little public attention, much less acknowledged. The story of its pain failed to penetrate into our hearts and minds. It remained buried and uncared for. This pushing back of the experience meant that many from the scene either died early or became sick. A number committed suicide. Bärbel Bohley, the female icon of the revolution, went to Croatia in 1996; Jürgen Fuchs died in 1999. In this way two driving forces behind East German resistance were no longer there. They left a gap that couldn't be filled again.

Dissidence in East Germany and its degrading fight for compensation and political pensions. Was there no other way? Those concerned had to stand by and watch the dominance with which the old elite reformed itself strategically after 1989. The public arena seemed like the ideal place for engaging again with the guiding principles of the East, be it in politics, culture or sport, this time in a different set of circumstances. The legendary East Germans were guaranteed media attention. Bruno Apitz, Täve Schur, Maxie Wander – they could always be wheeled out. But Edeltraud Eckert or Eveline Kuffel[1]? Has anyone heard of them? How about looking elsewhere? For the damaged and suppressed? Instead, the powers-that-be stuck to well-trodden paths and evidence-based frameworks: familiar names, elaborate discourse, accepted interpretations – all of this was internalized in the East German mind and stayed there. Ideological interests remained ideological interests.

---

[1] Marginalized East German writer.

LOOPING. The SED, as the old single state party that, through several name changes, restyled itself skilfully and vocally in the unified country as the protest movement from the East, denied the documentary evidence and a historical truth with which it had exploited the country for forty years. It seemed hardly to matter that the left took in a large number of Stasi people; no one really noticed the way they are still taunting their victims to this day; much too little was made of the fact that it was the left that explicitly failed to guide the East Germans towards democracy. It pretended to take care of things, it needed votes, it had a home advantage. Its systematic power strategists were mainly preoccupied with ensuring that the party could benefit from the same political looping that they themselves had managed to perform so effortlessly even in the new era. Was it possible in the years after the dictatorship, given the failed policies of the other parties, to pursue a more successful strategy? In retrospect it is also this political irresponsibility that paved the way for the AfD and made it so strong. To that extent, it was logical that the AfD should succeed the Left as a protest party in the East and that the left-wing Gregor Gysi should be succeeded there by the right-wing Alexander Gauland.

'Freedom is the possibility of resisting destiny,' as Vilém Flusser wrote. And it has to do with his destiny that for me this sentence could only go one way – it came out of the dark and sought the light. That is what gave it weight and urgency. For some time, however, I've had the feeling that that sentence has started to change direction. Freedom is also the possibility of opting for the dark side, for the pockets of toxicity in our history, in order to drag them back to the surface like streaky bubbles and leave them to take effect.

The diktat of the past century and its staying power. As if new life were being breathed into the things that defined our inner emotional spaces. As if something unfiltered were flowing into a wide river. The scattered endpoints, the unresolved elements, the remnants around which a society coalesces again. The armour of the war children, grandchildren, and great-grandchildren. The virtual world, the post-truth era, the festering concept of 'us', our destructive obsession, our orphaned experiences. It becomes purer, deeper, harder. Fury and freedom. East Germany as a condensate, a Petri dish of violence, a battleground. What's it all about?

EMPTY HOUSES. The pictures of 1 September 2018. The Chemnitz march of the neo-Nazi scene after the German-Cuban Daniel H. – called 'Negi' and long a target of right-wing violence – was injured so badly in a fight with a young Syrian that he died of the stab wounds. The speed with which the right-wing camp mobilized – AfD, Pegida, the Identitarian movement, Neue Rechte, Heimattreue Deutsche Jugend, the banned Nationale Sozialisten Chemnitz and all kinds of prominent right-wing politicians. The new representatives, the cohesion, the inner Hitler, the clear avowal. They sang the national anthem, linked arms, chanted 'We are the people', 'lying press', 'resistance', were demonstratively united, ruled the streets. It was about cultural hegemony. That day was to become an unequivocal symbol. No possibility of misunderstanding. A new war, open-ended.

They were led by Uwe Junge, Björn Höcke, Jörg Urban, Andreas Kalbitz, Siegfried Däbritz, Götz Kubitschek, Lutz Bachmann. All familiar media faces. Television images. In the fourth row, Michael – serious, determined. I knew him too well for me to ignore it. Why was he part of this 'national defensive struggle'? What had changed so definitively within him to make him act like this now? His family, as unspecific as mine. The father a party functionary in the GDR, aggressive, energetic, narcissist, work fetishist. The mother in the tax office, sighing, enigmatic, warm-hearted, crushed. Both war children. The son distant, critical, thoughtful, well-read. After 1989 his search for political answers, first with the Greens, then the FDP and finally the AfD. I wonder where he'll land in three years' time, when the next paradise is lost. 'We welcome illusions because they spare us unpleasurable feelings,' wrote Freud.

The search for the imaginary ideal. In Andrei Tarkovsky's first film *Ivan's Childhood*, the camera sweeps through the destruction of Berlin at the end of the war. The buildings have been bombed, the authority is gone. All that can be heard are the old haunting voices. After the end of the GDR, it was Heiner Müller who wrote from the mid-1990s about the 'emigration of authority into dream' and worked on the utopian dimension of communism. He had a feeling for abandoned houses, old identities, ruins, allegorical landscapes, the clinging century. The idiom of East Germany as an empty shell and its internalized victim role. The collective we, exploited and stunned. The unification nirvana and the huge fractures. The awareness among East Germans that even in a unified Germany they were still just outcasts and permanent losers. The West that couldn't be surpassed. One way or another, it remained the touchstone. The Left, which as the people's party of East Germany, was meant to absolve the East Germans but failed because it was so highly toxic itself. And then? How to fill an empty shell – and with what? The problem of the individual and mass society. East Germany had preached the great and necessary vision of a society that would replace the individual 'I' with the collective 'we'. There was no place for the 'I'; it didn't exist, it was decadent and should not appear. So now, how could we move from this mass collective consciousness towards the 'I'?

And then? Then came Merkel's refugee summer, which in the eyes of many East Germans revoked the principle of the welfare state in favour of refugee migrants. But integrate *us* first, was the slogan of the hour. A caesura that not only welded together anxious populists of all colours, but also triggered the entire spectrum of German emotions. Fear as political reality, as something that formed and was now able to unite Stasi people and victims of internment. Pain doesn't unite. What unites is ugly resentment.

MULTI-GENERATIONAL MOTTOS. Our experiences pick up speed. And at a meteoric rate. Twenty-five years after the 1989 revolution, a new East Germany formed out of the collective. Thousands of self-proclaimed 'Patriotic Europeans against the Islamization of the West' demonstrated on the streets. The initial pronouncements by Pegida ran roughly as follows: 'We are patriots, in other words the righteous ones. Those who are not like us must leave. Germany is going to the dogs, but we are here to rescue it.' They were passionate sports freaks, high earners who had finally gained a bit of status, disco heroes and rockers who were still somehow wearing their FDJ shirts underneath their leather jackets, some of them with a criminal record. A section of middle-class Saxony that had appointed itself as a movement. The slogans spewed out by the Pegida supporters sounded like multi-generational mottos. As if the sons were screaming out the words of their grandfathers and fathers and stopped only when everything had been disgorged. They were words that were somehow familiar: the old racist tone, the old hubris of the chosen. For a while it was: 'We are the underdogs. The East is the new cult. Now let's go and bash Wessis.' Pegida as the undead, as the alarmist barrel organ of defeatism, and baroque Dresden as a restoration stage for a self-radicalizing play. Later, the Pegida slogans became shriller and more determined: 'Germany, love it or leave it. If I could, I would call my people to arms.'

Pegida and the AfD. Formations with a lot to them. Eastern Germany is not a homogeneous block. In a family of AfD sympathizers, quite different types of people can sit together at the same table: from the apolitical to the political know-alls, from the latent xenophobes uninterested in the world to the well-travelled critics of capitalism. What unites them apart from globalization and a sensitive outer skin? What is their inner capital? Where are we? Pegida and the AfD, which absolve the East from having to face up to its own history. 'With spoon-fed politics, East Germans when in doubt will vote AfD,' was the headline in April 2018 in *Die Welt*. The populist wing of the AfD and its narrative of Germany's history, that strategically washes away the red lines of the West: the role of the Wehrmacht, the 'bird shit'.[2] Even more, the history of the GDR will soon cease to exist at all. Now it's about rewriting, discussion spaces, political power. This is most easily achieved through old nostalgic images: of the nation, the patriarchal family, Uncle Gauland, who styles himself as Uncle Sam, as guarantor for internal security against a scary, turbulent world. In Dresden the fear index doubled within a year from 2017 to 2018. 'The East on average has a conservative structure and values.' The AfD is well aware of this and overtly converts its outer consciousness into volatile political energy. It's about hate, which has long become something to experiment with. 'The socialization in the East is completely different,' explains Gauland. 'There we are a protest party and movement. In the West we are more of a liberal conservative reform party.'

The political principle is comparatively simple: the AfD in the East systematically plays on emotional fear. Refugees, Islam, Western hegemony, crime, sexual violence by foreigners. The narrower the political spectrum, the more it focuses on the East's fear of loss, and the more successful Gauland's party becomes. Fear as political trigger. In this vulnerable interaction, it continues to confirm the East's victim status and is even capable of developing it into a political power factor: 'We are the threatened majority, we are the opposition, we are on the threshold of a new era.' A policy of internal walls. Through this deal, the essence of red anti-fascism is reproduced and transformed into an ideal for the future, a new amalgamated

---

[2] Reference to a quote by Alexander Gauland, leader of the right-wing AfD: 'Hitler is just "a splatter of bird shit" in the history of Germany.'

East German identity: the individual as part of a collective, victim status, defiant regionalism, demarcation at last from the West, a 'strong, pure core Germany'.

In Potsdam after 1990, Gauland worked as the long-standing CDU state secretary from Chemnitz with inside knowledge of the political DNA of the West. For years he observed the dejection, insecurity and frustration of East German society. He was able to make good use of what he saw for his identity politics. Everything that is still politically unclear in the East readily finds a home in the AfD. A mainstream phenomenon, one of collective angst. It helps the East to exploit the German political landscape and prevents it from finding a way to become a responsible society. What is to be done to confront the violent history of the East in such a way that it can be relegated to the past? If the Federal Republic and National Socialism are the yardsticks, then the East is in the 1970s in terms of its memory politics. In the West at that time society was beginning to ask exactly what had happened under the Nazis and what fathers, aunts, grandfathers and mothers had to do with it.

East Germany and its history before 1989. If eastern Germany is finally to understand its own history, it will have to dig down before 1945 and lay it bare. How should this be done? Is it feasible at all? Wouldn't the West also give up in the face of such a mammoth historical task? It is too much at the moment to ask the East to emancipate itself from its dual experience of dictatorship. It is imploding into a political crisis, a disease, denial. And it's becoming more radical. The statistics in this regard cannot be ignored. Oliver Decker and Elmar Brähler, who have been carrying out research at the University of Leipzig since 2002 on the development of authoritarian and extreme right-wing mentalities, noted in their November 2018 study *Flucht ins Autoritäre* that half of East Germans are xenophobic. Moreover, one in two East Germans would like to ban Muslim migration. Decker and Brähler claim that the main origin of extreme right-wing positions is an authoritarian character, one that sympathizes with dictatorship, trivializes National Socialism and holds chauvinistic and social Darwinist views. In the East it is older persons who support an authoritarian right-wing dictatorship, whereas in the West it is more the younger ones. 'Conversely,' they say, 'this does not mean that all West Germans are democratically inclined.'

The collective of like-minded people. In his study *The Authoritarian Personality*, Theodor W. Adorno noted that the idea of exclusion 'depends on psychological needs'. He states: 'What people say and, to a lesser degree, what they really think depends very largely upon the climate of opinion in which they are living.' What is to be done? There will not be any simple or quick answers. Nothing has gone away, nothing has been sorted out, only time has passed. But perhaps at least that will help? The east of Germany needs a good place within itself, its own narrative, public recognition of its long painful history, differentiation, and its experiences must be externalized, in the political sphere, in education, but above all in the family.

BASIC. The thing with families, generational tensions, loyalties. The force of the upheavals after 1989, the chaos of structural reconstruction, the total collapse of the family demography. For years, births, marriages and divorces all slumped to historically low levels in the East. The family began to recover from the mid-1990s and became a stabilizing factor, an orientation, a bulwark and intimate pole of attraction against the huge sense of insecurity in the East. But what has happened at the micro-level within families? What has become of the silence in the private sphere? How have the threatened identities of parents and grandparents evolved? What has been queried, what has been clarified? How do the diffuse internal images now manifest themselves? Above all, how can people in the east of Germany escape from the family jungle – when psychoanalysis is only just re-establishing itself there?

The stories of those who left East Germany, the stories of those who returned there, the stories of the West Germans who began their lives after 1989 in the East. Who has adapted to whom? What has been added? 'Reverse migration is in the first instance a return to social networks such as the family,' says Tim Leibert of the Leibniz Institute in Leipzig, confirming the current trend of returning to the East. The reasons are to look after parents, to re-identify with the *heimat*, to reunite with friends, or to inherit real estate. With the young generation Y returnees, there is an additional aspect – a general, highly emotional defence of the East.

Robby, the person closest to me. The basic memories. Perhaps music was invented for them. It reaches us more directly and more equivocally. It gets to us. It gets under our skin. With words it's difficult. Not everything can or should be communicable. I sit in thought on his bed in the palliative ward at St. Joseph-Stift in Dresden. He tells me that from the beginning the school where he taught was the anti-Pegida school. That the resistance was organized from it. And that it wasn't over. It just needed to be resurrected. He smiles. He looks at me as he used to when he was a boy. He asks what I would call what's going on outside. We haven't spoken for so long, he says. We talk about it. He leans back and closes his eyes. It will be good, he says, to go to demonstrations together in spring. I've been so looking forward to that. I take his right hand. It's cold. He dozes off.

What do we know about what passes through our minds and why? When something suddenly occurs to us, makes itself known, needs to be said, when the inner defence mechanism is lowered so as to bring something out into the open? Robby sleeps. I hear a telephone ringing inside me, as if from far away. It is 12 May 2012. I can see myself going to the hall and picking up the phone. My brother's voice. It sounds serious. He doesn't know, he says, if it's right and whether he should, but it doesn't matter. He has to tell me. What? I ask. That father has died. Today? No just now, an hour ago. I listen to his words. I think that something must now come out. Something hidden, that wanted to be resurrected. He knows as well. There are these pauses that only we know and that we have never managed to bridge. Only we knew what they meant. Robby talks of Borussia Dortmund and Bayern Munich. That father was in the garden all day, that he chopped wood and mowed the lawn, that there was beer in the fridge, because he wanted to watch the cup final in Berlin that evening. He was looking forward to it. But then he said oh! and was dead.

Later, at father's funeral, the hidden still remains concealed. Robby gives the funeral oration. He says that father's life was intense, that it pushed the music into the background, that as leader of a large collective he had lots of responsibility, that he was also chosen for *more secret tasks* that his children knew nothing about and that he never talked about afterwards either. That's what he says. Really. I am still holding Robby's hand. It twitches slightly. I remember that that day was the last time we had seen one another. We had walked through the cemetery. Robby had given me his notes for the speech as we were saying farewell and asked me if I had liked it.

That was five years ago. No, six already. I read Robby's letters. And mine. I'm surprised how openly we had it out with one another. I'd forgotten that. He writes insistently about his positive suppression, and I about the averted gaze and the denial. Robby didn't want to talk about it. He stuck with the spectacular untruths in the family. Evidently he couldn't face up to them. What was hidden should remain unknown and no longer surface. There was something he didn't want to go into, our shared place. He wanted his story to be buried in the family crypt. We never resolved that. It wasn't possible. Sometimes I comfort myself with the thought that we just didn't have enough time. Sometimes I imagine where we would sit and talk, in ten, twenty years, even later.

I train myself outwardly, inwardly nothing changes. I want Robby to come running up the stairs, groan a bit, give me a fleeting kiss and start talking about something or other. I want him to be here. My life is still my life. I do what I've always done. I can see my brother smiling, I can hear him talking. I miss you.

Bibliography

Abraham, Nicolas and Torok, Maria, *The Wolf Man's Magic Word: A Cryptonymy*, trans. Nicholas Rand (Minneapolis: University of Minnesota Press, 2005)

Adorno, Theodor, *The Authoritarian Personality* (New York: Verso Books, 1950)

Angrik, Andrej and Klein, Peter, *The 'Final Solution' in Riga: Exploitation and Annihilation, 1941–1945*, trans. Ray Brandon (New York: Berghahn, 2009)

Apitz, Bruno, *Naked Among Wolves*, trans. Edith Anderson (Berlin: Seven Seas, 1960)

Arendt, Hannah, *Besuch in Deutschland* (Berlin: Rotbuch, 1993)

Assmann, Aleida and Harth, Dietrich (eds.), *Mnemosyne: Formen und Funktionen der kulturellen Erinnerung* (Frankfurt/M.: S. Fischer, 1991)

Bahrke, Ulrich (ed.), *'Denk ich an Deutschland. . .': Sozialpsychologische Reflexionen* (Frankfurt/M.: Brandes & Apsel-Verlag, 1990)

Bahrmann, Hannes and Links, Christoph, *Wir sind das Volk: Die DDR zwischen 7. Oktober und 17. Dezember 1989 – Eine Chronik* (Berlin: Aufbau, 1990)

Barthes, Roland, *Camera Lucida: Reflections on Photography*, trans. Richard Howard (New York: Hill and Wang, 1982)

Becker, Franziska, Merkel, Ina and Tippach-Scheider, Simone (eds.), *Das Kollektiv bin ich: Utopie und Alltag in der DDR* (Cologne: Böhlau, 2000)

Berth, Hendrik et al. (eds.), *Innenansichten der Transformation: 25 Jahre Sächsische Längsschnittstudie (1987–2012)* (Giessen: Psychosozial-Verlag, 2012)

Bohrer, Karl Heinz, *Ekstasen der Zeit: Augenblick, Gegenwart, Erinnerung* (Munich: Hanser, 2003)

Brauns, Dirk, *Im Inneren des Landes* (Berlin: Galiani, 2012)

Busch, Michael et al. (eds.), *Zwischen Prekarisierung und Protest: Die Lebenslagen und Generationsbilder von Jugendlichen in Ost und West* (Bielefeld: Transcript, 2010)

Canetti, Elias, *Über den Tod* (Munich: Hanser, 2014)

Chernivsky, Marina and Scheuring, Jana, *Gefühlserbschaften im Umbruch: Perspektiven, Kontroversen, Gegenwartsfragen* (Frankfurt/M.: Zentralwohlfahrtsstelle der Juden in Deutschland, 2016)

Crone, Katja and Schnepf, Robert (eds.), *Über die Seele* (Frankfurt/M.: Suhrkamp, 2010)

Denk, Felix and von Thülen, Sven, *Der Klang der Familie* (Berlin: Suhrkamp, 2012)

Derrida, Jacques, *Speech and Phenomena: And Other Essays on Husserl's Theory of Signs*, trans. David B. Allison (Evanston, IL: Northwestern University Press, 1973)

Didion, Joan, *The Year of Magical Thinking* (New York: Knopf, 2005)

Dürrschmidt, Jörg, *Rückkehr aus der Globalisierung? Der Heimkehrer als Sozialfigur der Moderne* (Hamburg: Hamburger Edition, 2013)

Flusser, Vilém, *The Freedom of the Migrant*, trans. Anke K. Finger (Champaign, IL: University of Illinois Press, 2013)

Flusser, Vilém, *Groundless*, trans. Rodrigo Maltez Novaes (Metaflux, 2017)

Foucault, Michel, *Le Corps utopique, Les Hétéropies: Suivi de Les hétéropies* (Fécamp: Éditions Lignes, 2019)

Geipel, Ines, *Generation Mauer: Ein Porträt* (Stuttgart: Klett-Cotta, 2014)

Geipel, Ines and Walther, Joachim, *Gesperrte Ablage: Unterdrückte Literaturgeschichte in Ostdeutschland 1945–1989* (Düsseldorf: Lilienfeld, 2015)

Grabbe, Katharina, Köhler, G. Sigrid and Wagner-Egelhaaf, Martina (eds.), *Das Imaginäre der Nation: Zur Persistenz einer politischen Kategorie* (Bielefeld: Transcript, 2012)

Grill, Andrea, *Schmetterlinge: Ein Porträt* (Berlin: Matthes & Seitz, 2016)

Gruen, Arno, *The Betrayal of the Self: The Fear of Autonomy in Men and Women*, trans. Hildegarde and Hunter Hannum (New York: Grove Press, 1988)

Gruen, Arno, *The Insanity of Normality: Realism as Sickness – Toward Understanding Human Destructiveness*, trans. Hildegarde and Hunter Hannum (New York: Grove Weidenfeld, 1992)

Grunenberg, Antonia, *Die Lust an der Schuld: Von der Macht der Vergangenheit über die Gegenwart* (Berlin: Rowohlt, 2001)

Grüning, Michael, *Der Wachsmann-Report: Auskünfte eines Architekten* (Berlin: Verlag der Nation, 1986)

Hacker, Michael, Maiwald, Stephanie and Staemmler, Johannes (eds.), *Dritte Generation Ost: Wer wir sind, was wir wollen* (Berlin: Christoph Links, 2012)

Halbwachs, Maurice, *On Collective Memory*, trans. Lewis A. Coser (Chicago: University of Chicago Press, 2020)

Herf, Jeffrey, *Divided Memory: The Nazi Past in the Two Germanys* (Cambridge, MA: Harvard University Press, 1999)

Heitmeyer, Wilhelm, *Autoritäre Versuchungen: Signaturen der Bedrohung* (Berlin: Suhrkamp, 2018)

Herrndorf, Wolfgang, *Arbeit und Struktur* (Berlin: Rowohlt, 2013)

Jureit, Ulrike, *Generationsforschung* (Giessen: Psychosozial-Verlag, 2006)

Kappelt, Olaf, *Braunbuch DDR – Nazis in der DDR* (Berlin: Historica, 2009)

Kertész, Imre, *Die exilierte Sprache: Essays und Reden* (Frankfurt/M.: Suhrkamp, 2004)

Kilian, Jürgen, *Krieg auf Kosten anderer: Das Reichsministerium für Finanzen und die wirtschaftliche Mobilisierung Europas für Hitlers Krieg* (Berlin: De Gruyter Oldenbourg, 2017)

Koenen, Gerd, *Vesper, Ensslin, Baader: Urszenen des deutschen Terrorismus* (Frankfurt/M.: S. Fischer, 2005)

Kowalczuk, Ilko-Sascha, *End Game: The 1989 Revolution in East Germany*, trans. Patricia C. Sutcliffe (New York: Berghahn, 2022)

Kuhlemann, Jens, *Braune Kader: Ehemalige Nationalsozialisten in der Deutschen Wirtschaftskommission und der DDR-Regierung (1948–1957)* (Norderstedt: Books on Demand, 2014)

Leonhard, Wolfgang, *Child of the Revolution*, trans. C.M. Woodhouse (London: Collins, 1957)

Lethen, Helmut, *Der Sound der Väter: Gottfried Benn und seine Zeit* (Berlin: Rowohlt, 2006)

Lethen, Helmut, *Der Schatten des Fotografen: Bilder und ihre Wirklichkeit* (Berlin: Rowohlt, 2014)

Lindau, Ursula, *Der Schrei und die Stille: Trauer und Tod bei Künstlern der Klassischen Moderne* (Husum: Uhleo, 2018)

Lohl, Jan and Moré, Angela, *Unbewusste Erbschaften des Nationalsozialismus: Psychoanalytische, sozialpsychologische und historische Studien* (Giessen: Psychosozial-Verlag, 2014)

Maaz, Hans-Joachim, *Der Gefühlsstau: Ein Psychogramm der DDR* (Berlin: Argon, 1990)

Mallmann, Klaus-Michael (ed.), *Karrieren der Gewalt: Nationalsozialistische Täterbiographien* (Darmstadt: Wissenschaftliche Buchgesellschaft, 2011)

Micus-Loos, Christiane, *Bildung, Indentität, Geschichte: Ost- und westdeutsche Generationserfahrungen im Spiegel autobiographischer Texte* (Paderborn: Schöningh, 2012)

Mitscherlich, Alexander and Margarete, *The Inability to Mourn: Principles of Collective Behavior*, trans. Beverley R. Placzek (New York: Grove Press, 1975)

Müller, Heiner, *Gesamtausgabe: Die Gedichte – Werke 1* (Frankfurt/M.: Suhrkamp, 1998)

Müller, Uwe and Hartmann, Grit, *Vorwärts und vergessen! Kader, Spitzel und Komplizen: Das gefährliche Erbe der SED-Diktatur* (Berlin: Rowohlt, 2009)

Niethammer, Lutz (ed.) et al., *Der 'gesäuberte' Antifaschismus: Die SED und die roten Kapos von Buchenwald – Dokumente* (Berlin: Akademie-Verlag, 1994)

Pingel-Schliemann, Sandra, *Zersetzen: Strategie einer Diktatur* (Berlin: Robert-Havemann-Gesellschaft, 2004)

Plänkers, Tomas and Bahrke, Ulrich (eds.), *Seele und totalitärer Staat: Zur psychischen Erbschaft der DDR* (Giessen: Psychosozial-Verlag, 2005)

Reulecke, Jürgen, *Generationalität und Lebensgeschichte im 20. Jahrhundert* (Munich: Oldenbourg Wissenschaftsverlag, 2003)

Sabrow, Martin (ed.), *Autobiographische Aufarbeitung: Diktatur und Legbensgeschichte im 20. Jahrhundert* (Leipzig: Akademische Verlagsanstalt, 2012)

Schivelbusch, Wolfgang, *The Culture of Defeat: On National Trauma, Mourning and Recovery*, trans. Jefferson Chase (New York: Picador, 2003)

Schmeitzner, Mike, *Schulen der Diktatur: Die Kaderausbuldung der KPD/SED in Sachsen 1945–1952* (Dresden: Hannah-Arendt-Institut für Totalitarismusforschung, 2001)

Schüle, Annegret et al., *Die DDR aus generationenge-schichtlicher Perspective: Eine Inventur* (Leipzig: Leipziger Universitätsverlag, 2006)

Seegers, Lu and Reulecke, Jürgen (eds.), *Die Generation der Kriegskinder: Historische Hintergründe und Deutungen* (Giessen: Psychosozial-Verlag, 2009)

Seidler, Christoph and Froese, Michael J., *Traumatisierungen in (Ost-)Deutschland* (Giessen: Psychosozial-Verlag, 2006)

Sloterdijk, Peter, *Kopernikanische Mobilmachung und ptolemäische Abrüstung* (Frankfurt/M.: Suhrkamp, 1987)

Sloterdijk, Peter and Heinrichs, Hans-Jürgen, *Neither Sun nor Death*, trans. Steven Corcoran (Los Angeles: Semiotext(e), 2011)

Snyder, Timothy, *The Road to Unfreedom: Russia, Europe, America* (London: Bodley Head, 2018)

Sofsky, Wolfgang, *Violence: Terrorism, Genocide, War*, trans. Anthea Bell (London: Granta Books, 2003)

Sundermeyer, Olaf, *Gauland: Die Rache des alten Mannes* (Munich: C.H. Beck, 2018)

Theweleit, Klaus, *Male Fantasies*, trans. Stephen Conway et al. (Cambridge: Polity Press, 1987)

Thomése, P. F., *Shadow Child*, trans. Sam Garrett (London: Trafalgar Square, 2005)

Trobisch-Lüge, Stefan, *Das späte Gift: Folgen politischer Traumatisierungen in der DDR und ihre Behandlung* (Giessen: Psychosozial-Verlag, 2004)

Ullmann, Linn, *Unquiet: A Novel*, trans. Thilo Reinhard (New York: W.W. Norton & Company, 2019)

Vamik, D. Volkan, *Das Versagen der Diplomatie: Zur Psychoanalyse nationaler, ethnischer und religiöser Konflikte* (Giessen: Psychosozial-Verlag, 1999)

Wagner, Thomas, *Die Angstmacher: 1968 und die Neuen Rechten* (Berlin: Aufbau, 2017)

Waibel, Harry, *Die Braune Saat: Antisemitismus und Neonazismus in der DDR* (Stuttgart: Schmetterling, 2017)

Wendler, Fabian, *National Socialist-Täter in der Geschichtsschreibung der SBZ und DDR bis in die 1960-er Jahre* (Berlin: Metropol, 2017)

Wildt, Michael, *Generation der Unbedingten: Das Führungskorps des Reichssicherheitshauptamtes* (Hamburg: Hamburger Edition, 2003)

Yendell, Alexander, Pickel, Gert and Dörner, Karolin (eds.), *Innere Sicherheit in Sachsen: Beiträge zu einer kontroversen Debatte* (Leipzig: Edition Leipzig, 2017)